D1226557

MORNING AND EVENING PRAYER

Morning and Evening
PRAYER

Selections from *The Liturgy of the Hours*

Editors
REV. D. JOSEPH FINNERTY
REV. GEORGE J. RYAN

The Official Prayer of the Church
Edited for Popular Use

REGINA PRESS   **NEW YORK**

Nihil Obstat: Rev. Joseph L. Cunningham, S.T.L.
                      Diocesan Censor

Imprimatur: ✠   Francis J. Mugavero, D.D.
                      Bishop of Brooklyn

Reprinted, April 1985

Originally published by Regina Press 1978.

9 8 7 6 5 4 3

CONTENTS

The Canticle of Zechariah and the Canticle of Mary will be found inside the front and back covers, respectively.

FOREWORD

The Liturgy of the Hours has been restored as the public and common prayer of the Church. It is not meant to be the preserve of religious and clergy but should be made available to all people so that the "whole course of the day and night is made holy by the praises of God" (Const. on Lit. #84).

People have never really had access to morning and evening prayer from the Liturgy on a regular basis mostly because of the cost and complexity of the prayer books formerly called the *Divine Office*.

The present volume is far from the ideal of a sung common prayer. The editors recognize this ideal but have provided this volume as an initial step to its achievement. It is hoped that the faithful using this book will be motivated to use *Christian Prayer* containing the complete texts for morning and evening prayer and will be instrumental in leading groups in sung communal celebrations.

Recognizing the desire many have to pray the Liturgy of the Hours, this volume contains a simple format for the major seasons of the year. It is specifically designed for individual rather than communal celebrations so personal intentions may be added during the Intercessions and moments of reflection are encouraged after the Readings. There is no need for page turning and the gospel canticles are conveniently located inside the covers.

INTRODUCTION

In addition to the Eucharist and the other sacraments, the Church's official worship also includes the Liturgy of the Hours. In this post Vatican II age when many familiar devotions have disappeared, a serious difficulty has emerged for some people who have nothing to put in their place. Now, thanks to the leadership of Pope Paul VI and his brother bishops, what used to be called the *Breviary* or the *Divine Office,* has been restored to the entire church as a daily book of prayer called *The Liturgy of the Hours.*

A proper liturgical restoration of the Eucharist is guaranteed if it is associated with the Liturgy of the Hours. We can go a long way toward fostering mature eucharistic piety if it is supported by the daily prayer of the Church which continues the eucharistic themes of praise and thanksgiving throughout the day. The Eucharist is an act of worship that must be prepared for as well as lovingly and prayerfully recalled as the Christian's day or week unfolds. A harmony exists between Liturgy of the Hours and the Mass so that devotion for the Liturgy of the Hours inspires renewed devotion for the Mass.

The Church has prayed the Liturgy of the Hours over the centuries to allow its members to enter into the mind of Christ. The prayer life of Jesus, in addition to being personal and private was also public and communal. He prayed mornings and evenings in the synagogue with his fellow Israelites and disciples. The psalms, the scriptures, and other prayers became the school of piety that nourished him. This practice of Jesus was passed on to early Christians who spread it across the world and further developed it through the centuries.

With the reform of Paul VI the riches of the Liturgy of the Hours are no longer restricted to religious and clergy. It is the prayer of all Christians. Bishops and pastors have the responsibility of moving it from a strictly private recitation to a truly liturgical experience celebrated in common, sanctifying the hours of the day especially morning and evening.

Unfortunately, most Christians because of lifestyle, employment, sickness or other daily demands find it impossible to gather each day to sing the Liturgy of the Hours in community. Hopefully, this small book will meet the needs of those who wish to have a selection of the Church's daily prayer for their own morning and evening use. It can be prayed while travelling to or from work, in the quiet of a church or in one's home.

The structure of Morning and Evening Prayer is as follows:

1. Introductory verse.

2. Hymns. (Hymns have been included in an appendix for optional use.)

3. Psalm, canticle and psalm for morning prayer. Psalm, psalm and canticle for evening prayer. Antiphons to set the theme. A prayer to conclude each psalm.

4. Scripture reading followed by a period of reflection.

5. Gospel canticle found inside the covers:
for morning prayer—the Canticle of Zechariah;
for evening prayer—the Canticle of the Blessed Virgin Mary.

6. Intercessions.

7. Lord's Prayer.

8. Concluding Prayer.

9. Blessing.

An attempt has been made to provide a selection of morning and evening prayers for each of the liturgical seasons as well as the season throughout the year:

—For the liturgical season called "Ordinary Time", a morning and evening prayer has been provided for each day of the week.

—For Advent two selections are provided, which may be alternated on a daily or weekly basis.

—For Christmas there is one office which may be prayed on Christmas until the Baptism of the Lord.

—For Lent, there are three selections, the first is suggested for Sundays; the other two may be alternated on weekdays.

—For Easter there are two selections which may be alternated on a daily or weekly basis.

—For Pentecost there is one selection which may be said on the Feast itself and on days when one might wish to pray to the Holy Spirit.

Two additional selections have been provided for devotion. One in honor of the Blessed Virgin Mary which can be prayed on Saturdays or on any of her feasts. The other selection is for the dead. This can be used on the Feast of All Souls and when one feels the need to reflect on the mystery of death especially on the occasion of the death of a relative or friend.

Since the hymns in the Liturgy of the Hours are designed to be sung not recited, they have been included in this volume by way of *Appendix*. If an individual finds it prayerful on some occasions to include the hymn, it is to be inserted after the Introductory verse. Hymns appropriate to the season should be chosen. When celebrated in common, the hymn is never omitted.

Advent Season

. . . increase our longing for
Christ our Savior . . .

THIS SECTION MAY BE PRAYED
FROM THE FIRST SUNDAY OF ADVENT
TO CHRISTMAS EVE

MORNING PRAYER

God, come to my assistance.
—Lord, make haste to help me.

Glory to the Father, and to the Son, and to
   the Holy Spirit:
as it was in the beginning, is now, and will
   be for ever. Amen. Alleluia.

PSALMODY

Ant. 1   Stir up your mighty power, Lord; come to
         our aid.

Psalm 80
Lord, come, take care of your vineyard

Come, Lord Jesus (Revelation 22:20).

O shepherd of Israel, hear us,
you who lead Joseph's flock,
shine forth from your cherubim throne
upon Ephraim, Benjamin, Manasseh.
O Lord, rouse up your might,
O Lord, come to our help.

God of hosts, bring us back;
let your face shine on us and we shall be saved.

Lord God of hosts, how long
will you frown on your people's plea?

You have fed them with tears for their bread,
an abundance of tears for their drink.
You have made us the taunt of our neighbors,
our enemies laugh us to scorn.

God of hosts, bring us back;
let your face shine on us, and we shall be
saved.

You brought a vine out of Egypt;
to plant it you drove out the nations.
Before it you cleared the ground;
it took root and spread through the land.

The mountains were covered with its shadow,
the cedars of God with its boughs.
It stretched out its branches to the sea,
to the Great River it stretched out its shoots.

Then why have you broken down its walls?
It is plucked by all who pass by.
It is ravaged by the boar of the forest,
devoured by the beasts of the field.

God of hosts, turn again, we implore,
look down from heaven and see.

Visit this vine and protect it,
the vine your right hand has planted.
Men have burnt it with fire and destroyed it.
May they perish at the frown of your face.

May your hand be on the man you have cho-
    sen,
the man you have given your strength.
And we shall never forsake you again:
give us life that we may call upon your name.

God of hosts, bring us back;
let your face shine on us and we shall be saved.

Psalm-prayer

Lord God, eternal shepherd, you so tend the
vineyard you planted that now it extends its
branches even to the farthest coast. Look down
on your Church and come to us. Help us remain
in your Son as branches on the vine, that,
planted firmly in your love, we may testify before the whole world to your great power working everywhere.

Ant. 2   **The Lord has worked marvels for us;**
           make it known to the ends of the world.

CANTICLE   *Isaiah 12:1–6*
      Joy of God's ransomed people

If anyone thirsts, let him come to me and drink
(John 7:37).

    I give you thanks, O Lord;
    though you have been angry with me,

your anger has abated, and you have consoled
   me.

God indeed is my savior;
I am confident and unafraid.
My strength and my courage is the Lord,
and he has been my savior.

With joy you will draw water
at the fountain of salvation, and say on that
   day:
Give thanks to the Lord, acclaim his name;
among the nations make known his deeds,
proclaim how exalted is his name.

Sing praise to the Lord for his glorious
   achievement;
let this be known throughout all the earth.

Shout with exultation, O city of Zion,
for great in your midst
is the Holy One of Israel!

Ant. 3   Ring out your joy to God our strength.

Psalm 81
Solemn renewal of the Covenant

See that no one among you has a faithless heart
(Hebrews 3:12).

Ring out your joy to God our strength,
shout in triumph to the God of Jacob.

Raise a song and sound the timbrel,
the sweet-sounding harp and the lute,
blow the trumpet at the new moon,
when the moon is full, on our feast.

For this is Israel's law,
a command of the God of Jacob.
He imposed it as a rule on Joseph,
when he went out against the land of Egypt.

A voice I did not know said to me:
"I freed your shoulder from the burden;
your hands were freed from the load.
You called in distress and I saved you.

I answered, concealed in the storm cloud,
at the waters of Meribah I tested you.
Listen, my people, to my warning,
O Israel, if only you would heed!

Let there be no foreign god among you,
no worship of an alien god.
I am the Lord your God,
who brought you from the land of Egypt.
Open wide your mouth and I will fill it.

But my people did not heed my voice
and Israel would not obey,
so I left them in their stubbornness of heart
to follow their own designs.

O that my people would heed me,
that Israel would walk in my ways!
At once I would subdue their foes,
turn my hand against their enemies.

The Lord's enemies would cringe at their feet
and their subjection would last for ever.
But Israel I would feed with finest wheat
and fill them with honey from the rock."

Psalm-prayer

Lord God, open our mouths to proclaim your glory. Help us to leave sin behind and to rejoice in professing your name.

READING   *Isaiah 45:8*

Let justice descend, O heavens, like dew from above,
    like gentle rain let the skies drop it down.
Let the earth open and salvation bud forth;
    let justice also spring up!

RESPONSORY

Your light will come, Jerusalem;
the Lord will dawn on you in radiant beauty.
—Your light will come, Jerusalem;
the Lord will dawn on you in radiant beauty.

You will see his glory within you;
—the Lord will dawn on you in radiant beauty.

Glory to the Father . . .
—Your light will . . .

CANTICLE OF ZECHARIAH

Ant. I will help you, says the Lord. I am your
Savior, the Holy One of Israel.

INTERCESSIONS

Let us pray to God our Father who sent his Son
to save mankind:
Show us your mercy, Lord!
Father most merciful, we confess our faith in
your Christ with our words,
—keep us from denying him in our actions.
You have sent your Son to rescue us,
—remove every sorrow from the face of the
earth and from our country.
Our land looks forward with delight to the approach of your Son,
—let it experience the fullness of your joy.
Through your mercy make us live holy and
chaste lives in this world,
—eagerly awaiting the blessed hope and coming of Christ in glory.

Our Father . . .

PRAYER

Almighty Father,
give us the joy of your love
to prepare the way for Christ our Lord.
Help us to serve you and one another.

We ask this through our Lord Jesus Christ,
   your Son,
who lives and reigns with you and the Holy
   Spirit,
one God, for ever and ever.

May the Lord bless us,
protect us from all evil
and bring us to everlasting life.
—Amen.

EVENING PRAYER

God, come to my assistance.
—Lord, make haste to help me.

Glory to the Father, and to the Son, and to the
    Holy Spirit:
as it was in the beginning, is now, and will be
    for ever. Amen. Alleluia.

PSALMODY

Ant. 1 To you, O Lord, I lift up my soul; come
    and rescue me, for you are my refuge
    and my strength.

Psalm 132
God's promises to the house of David

The Lord God will give him the throne of his
ancestor David (Luke 1:32).

I

O Lord, remember David
and all the many hardships he endured,
the oath he swore to the Lord,
his vow to the Strong One of Jacob.

"I will not enter the house where I live
nor go to the bed where I rest.
I will give no sleep to my eyes,

to my eyelids I will give no slumber
till I find a place for the Lord,
a dwelling for the Strong One of Jacob."

At Ephrathah we heard of the ark;
we found it in the plains of Yearim.
"Let us go to the place of his dwelling;
let us go to kneel at his footstool."

Go up, Lord, to the place of your rest,
you and the ark of your strength.
Your priests shall be clothed with holiness:
your faithful shall ring out their joy.
For the sake of David your servant
do not reject your anointed.

Ant. 2   Bless those, O Lord, who have waited for
         your coming; let your prophets be
         proved true.

II

The Lord swore an oath to David;
he will not go back on his word:
"A son, the fruit of your body,
will I set upon your throne.

If they keep my covenant in truth
and my laws that I have taught them,
their sons also shall rule
on your throne from age to age."

For the Lord has chosen Zion;
he has desired it for his dwelling:
"This is my resting-place for ever,
here have I chosen to live.

I will greatly bless her produce,
I will fill her poor with bread.
I will clothe her priests with salvation
and her faithful shall ring out their joy.

There David's stock will flower:
I will prepare a lamp for my anointed.
I will cover his enemies with shame
but on him my crown shall shine."

Psalm-prayer

Lord Jesus Christ, you chose to suffer and be overwhelmed by death in order to open the gates of death in triumph. Stay with us to help us on our pilgrimage; free us from all evil by the power of your resurrection. In the company of your saints, and constantly remembering your love for us, may we sing of your wonders in our Father's house.

Ant. 3   Turn to us, O Lord, make haste to help
         your people.

CANTICLE   *Revelation 11:17–18; 12:10b–12a*
The judgment of God

We praise you, the Lord God Almighty,
who is and who was.
You have assumed your great power,
you have begun your reign.

The nations have raged in anger,
but then came your day of wrath
and the moment to judge the dead:
the time to reward your servants the prophets
and the holy ones who revere you,
the great and the small alike.

Now have salvation and power come,
the reign of our God and the authority
of his Anointed One.
For the accuser of our brothers is cast out,
who night and day accused them before God.

They defeated him by the blood of the Lamb
and by the word of their testimony;
love for life did not deter them from death.
So rejoice, you heavens,
and you that dwell therein!

READING   *Philippians 4:4–7*

Rejoice in the Lord always! I say it again. Rejoice! Everyone should see how unselfish you are. The Lord is near. Dismiss all anxiety from

your minds. Present your needs to God in every
form of prayer and in petitions full of gratitude.
Then God's own peace, which is beyond all un-
derstanding, will stand guard over your hearts
and minds, in Christ Jesus.

RESPONSORY

Lord, show us your mercy and love.
—Lord, show us your mercy and love.

And grant us your salvation,
—your mercy and love.

Glory to the Father . . .
—Lord, show us . . .

CANTICLE OF MARY

Ant. O sacred Lord of ancient Israel, who
     showed yourself to Moses in the burning
     bush, who gave him the holy law on Sinai
     mountain: come, stretch out your mighty
     hand to set us free.

INTERCESSIONS

To Christ the Lord, who was born of the Virgin
    Mary, let us pray with joyful hearts:
Come, Lord Jesus!
Lord Jesus, in the mystery of your incarnation,
    you revealed your glory to the world,

—give us new life by your coming.
You have taken our weaknesses upon yourself,
—grant us your mercy.
You redeemed the world from sin by your first
    coming in humility,
—free us from all guilt when you come again
    in glory.
You live and rule over all,
—in your goodness bring us to our eternal in-
    heritance.
You sit at the right hand of the Father,
—gladden the souls of the dead with your light.

Our Father . . .

PRAYER

All-powerful God,
renew us by the coming feast of your Son
and free us from our slavery to sin.

Grant this through our Lord Jesus Christ, your
    Son,
who lives and reigns with you and the Holy
    Spirit,
one God, for ever and ever.

May the Lord bless us,
protect us from all evil
and bring us to everlasting life.
—Amen.

MORNING PRAYER

God, come to my assistance.
—Lord, make haste to help me.

Glory to the Father, and to the Son, and to the
   Holy Spirit:
as it was in the beginning, is now, and will be
   for ever. Amen. Alleluia.

PSALMODY

Ant. 1   The Lord will come from his holy place
         to save his people.

Psalm 85
Our salvation is near

*God blessed the land when our Savior came to
earth* (Origen).

O Lord, you once favored your land
and revived the fortunes of Jacob,
you forgave the guilt of your people—

and covered all their sins.
You averted all your rage,
you calmed the heat of your anger.

Revive us now, God, our helper!
Put an end to your grievance against us.
Will you be angry with us for ever,
will your anger never cease?

17

Will you not restore again our life
that your people may rejoice in you?
Let us see, O Lord, your mercy
and give us your saving help.

I will hear what the Lord God has to say,
a voice that speaks of peace,
peace for his people and his friends
and those who turn to him in their hearts.
His help is near for those who fear him
and his glory will dwell in our land.

Mercy and faithfulness have met;
justice and peace have embraced.
Faithfulness shall spring from the earth
and justice look down from heaven.

The Lord will make us prosper
and our earth shall yield its fruit.
Justice shall march before him
and peace shall follow his steps.

Psalm-prayer

Show us your mercy, Lord; our misery is
known to us. May no evil desires prevail over
us, for your glory and love dwell in our hearts.
Amen

Ant. 2   Zion is our mighty citadel, our saving
         Lord its wall and its defense; throw open

the gates, for our God is here among us,
alleluia.

CANTICLE   *Isaiah 26:1–4, 7–9, 12*
Hymn after the defeat of the enemy

The city wall had twelve foundation stones (see
Revelation 21:14).

A strong city have we;
he sets up walls and ramparts to protect us.
Open up the gates
to let in a nation that is just,
one that keeps faith.

A nation of firm purpose you keep in peace;
in peace, for its trust in you.
Trust in the Lord forever!
For the Lord is an eternal Rock.

The way of the just is smooth;
the path of the just you make level.
Yes, for your way and your judgments, O Lord,
we look to you;
your name and your title
are the desire of our souls.

My soul yearns for you in the night,
yes, my spirit within me keeps vigil for you;
when your judgment dawns upon the earth,
the world's inhabitants learn justice.

O Lord, you mete out peace to us,
for it is you who have accomplished all we
   have done.

Ant. 3   **Lord, make known your will throughout
the earth; proclaim your salvation to
every nation.**

Psalm 67
People of all nations will worship the Lord

You must know that God is offering his salvation to all the world (Acts 28:28).

O God, be gracious and bless us
and let your face shed its light upon us.
So will your ways be known upon earth
and all nations learn your saving help.

Let the peoples praise you, O God;
let all the peoples praise you.

Let the nations be glad and exult
for you rule the world with justice.
With fairness you rule the peoples,
you guide the nations on earth.

Let the peoples praise you, O God;
let all the peoples praise you.

The earth has yielded its fruit
for God, our God, has blessed us.

May God still give us his blessing
till the ends of the earth revere him.

Let the peoples praise you, O God;
let all the peoples praise you.

Psalm-prayer

Be gracious and bless us, Lord, and let your
face shed its light on us, so that we can make you
known with reverence and bring forth a harvest
of justice.

READING   *Romans 13:11–14*

It is now the hour for you to wake from sleep,
for our salvation is closer than when we first
accepted the faith. The night is far spent; the day
draws near. Let us cast off deeds of darkness and
put on the armor of light. Let us live honorably
as in daylight; not in carousing and drunken-
ness, not in sexual excess and lust, not in quar-
reling and jealousy. Rather, put on the Lord
Jesus Christ and make no provision for the
desires of the flesh.

RESPONSORY

Your light will come, Jerusalem;
the Lord will dawn on you in radiant beauty.
—Your light will come, Jerusalem;
the Lord will dawn on you in radiant beauty.

You will see his glory within you;
—the Lord will dawn on you in radiant beauty.

Glory to the Father . . .
—Your light will . . .

CANTICLE OF ZECHARIAH

Ant.   Let everything within you watch and wait,
for the Lord our God draws near.

INTERCESSIONS

To the Lord Jesus Christ, judge of the living
and the dead, let us pray:
Come, Lord Jesus!
Lord Jesus, you came to save sinners,
—protect us in times of temptation.
You will come in glory to be our judge,
—show in us your power to save.
Help us to keep the precepts of your law with
the strength of the Spirit,
—and to look forward in love to your coming.
You are praised throughout the ages; in your
mercy help us to live devoutly and temper-
ately in this life,
—as we wait in joyful hope for the revelation
of your glory.

Our Father . . .

PRAYER

All-powerful God,
renew us by the coming feast of your Son
and free us from our slavery to sin.

Grant this through our Lord Jesus Christ, your
   Son,
who lives and reigns with you and the Holy
   Spirit,
one God, for ever and ever.

May the Lord bless us,
protect us from all evil
and bring us to everlasting life.
—Amen.

EVENING PRAYER

God, come to my assistance.
—Lord, make haste to help me.

Glory to the Father, and to the Son, and to the
   Holy Spirit:
as it was in the beginning, is now, and will be
   for ever. Amen. Alleluia.

PSALMODY

Ant. 1   The Lord, the mighty God, will come
         forth from Zion to set his people free.

Psalm 126
Joyful hope in God

*Just as you share in sufferings so you will share
in the divine glory* (2 Corinthians 1:7).

When the Lord delivered Zion from bondage,
it seemed like a dream.
Then was our mouth filled with laughter,
on our lips there were songs.

The heathens themselves said: "What marvels
the Lord worked for them!"
What marvels the Lord worked for us!
Indeed we were glad.

Deliver us, O Lord, from our bondage
as streams in dry land.

Those who are sowing in tears
will sing when they reap.

They go out, they go out, full of tears,
carrying seed for the sowing:
they come back, they come back, full of song,
carrying their sheaves.

Psalm-prayer

Lord, you have raised us from the earth;
may you let the seeds of justice, which we
have sown in tears, grow and increase in your
sight. May we reap in joy the harvest we hope
for patiently.

Ant. 2   I shall not cease to plead with God for
Zion until he sends his Holy One in all
his radiant beauty.

Psalm 127
Apart from God our labors are worthless

You are God's building (1 Corinthians 3:9).

If the Lord does not build the house,
in vain do its builders labor;
if the Lord does not watch over the city,
in vain does the watchman keep vigil.

In vain is your earlier rising,
your going later to rest,
you who toil for the bread you eat:

when he pours gifts on his beloved while they
  slumber.

Truly sons are a gift from the Lord,
a blessing, the fruit of the womb.
Indeed the sons of youth
are like arrows in the hand of a warrior.

O the happiness of the man
who has filled his quiver with these arrows!
He will have no cause for shame
when he disputes with his foes in the gate-
  ways.

Psalm-prayer

You command the seed to rise, Lord God,
though the farmer is unaware. Grant that those
who labor for you may trust not in their own
work but in your help. Remembering that the
land is brought to flower not with human tears
but with those of your Son, may the Church rely
only upon your gifts.

> The Spirit of the Lord rests upon me; he
> has sent me to preach his joyful message
> to the poor.

CANTICLE   *Colossians 1:12–20*
Christ the first-born of all creation and the
        first-born from the dead

Let us give thanks to the Father
for having made you worthy
to share the lot of the saints
in light.

He rescued us
from the power of darkness
and brought us
into the kingdom of his beloved Son.
Through him we have redemption,
the forgiveness of our sins.

He is the image of the invisible God,
the first-born of all creatures.
In him everything in heaven and on earth was
   created,
things visible and invisible.

All were created through him;
all were created for him.
He is before all else that is.
In him everything continues in being.

It is he who is head of the body, the church!
he who is the beginning,
the first-born of the dead,
so that primacy may be his in everything.

It pleased God to make absolute fullness reside
   in him—

and, by means of him, to reconcile everything
  in his person,
both on earth and in the heavens,
making peace through the blood of his cross.

READING   *James 5:7–11*

Be patient, my brothers, until the coming of
the Lord. See how the farmer awaits the precious yield of the soil. He looks forward to it patiently while the soil receives the winter and the
spring rains. You, too, must be patient. Steady
your hearts, because the coming of the Lord is at
hand. Do not grumble against one another, my
brothers, lest you be condemned. See! The judge
stands at the gate. As your models in suffering
hardships and in patience, brothers, take the
prophets who spoke in the name of the Lord.
Those who have endured we call blessed. You
have heard of the steadfastness of Job, and have
seen what the Lord, who is compassionate and
merciful, did in the end.

RESPONSORY

Come and set us free, Lord God of power and
  might.
—Come and set us free, Lord God of power and
  might.

Let your face shine upon us and we shall be
  saved,
—Lord God of power and might.

Glory to the Father . . .
—Come and set . . .

CANTICLE OF MARY

Ant. O King of all the nations, the only joy of
      every human heart; O Keystone of the
      mighty arch of man, come and save the
      creature you fashioned from the dust.

INTERCESSIONS

To Christ our Lord, who humbled himself for
  our sake, we joyfully say:
      Come, Lord Jesus!
Lord Jesus, by your coming you rescued the
  world from sin,
—cleanse our souls and bodies from guilt.
By the mystery of your incarnation we are
  made your brothers and sisters,
—do not let us become estranged from you.
Do not judge harshly,
—those you redeemed with such great cost.

No age, O Christ, is without your goodness and
  holy riches,

—enable us to merit the enduring crown of your glory.

Lord, to you we commend the souls of your departed servants,

—having died to the world, may they be alive in you for ever.

Our Father . . .

PRAYER

God our Father,
you sent your Son
to free mankind from the power of death.
May we who celebrate the coming of Christ as man
share more fully in his divine life,
for he lives and reigns with you and the Holy Spirit,
one God, for ever and ever.

May the Lord bless us,
protect us from all evil
and bring us to everlasting life.
—Amen.

Christmas Season

*. . . may we bring your life
to the waiting world . . .*

**THIS SECTION MAY BE PRAYED
FROM CHRISTMAS DAY
TO THE BAPTISM OF THE LORD**

MORNING PRAYER

God, come to my assistance.
—Lord, make haste to help me.

Glory to the Father, and to the Son, and to the
    Holy Spirit:
as it was in the beginning, is now, and will be
    for ever. Amen. Alleluia.

PSALMODY

Ant. 1   Tell us, shepherds, what have you seen?
           Who has appeared on earth? We have
           seen a newborn infant and a choir of
           angels praising the Lord, alleluia.

Psalm 63:2–9
A soul thirsting for God

Whoever has left the darkness of sin yearns for
God.

O God, you are my God, for you I long;
for you my soul is thirsting.
My body pines for you
like a dry, weary land without water.
So I gaze on you in the sanctuary
to see your strength and your glory.

For your love is better than life,
my lips will speak your praise.

33

So I will bless you all my life,
in your name I will lift up my hands.
My soul shall be filled as with a banquet,
my mouth shall praise you with joy.

On my bed I remember you.
On you I muse through the night
for you have been my help;
in the shadow of your wings I rejoice.
My soul clings to you;
your right hand holds me fast.

Psalm-prayer

Father, creator of unfailing light, give that same light to those who call to you. May our lips praise you; our lives proclaim your goodness; our work give you honor, and our voices celebrate you for ever.

Ant. 2   The angel said to the shepherds: I proclaim to you a great joy; today the Savior of the world is born for you, alleluia.

CANTICLE   *Daniel 3:57–88, 56*
Let all creatures praise the Lord

All you servants of the Lord, sing praise to him (Revelation 19:5).

Bless the Lord, all you works of the Lord.
Praise and exalt him above all forever.

Angels of the Lord, bless the Lord.
You heavens, bless the Lord.
All you waters above the heavens, bless the
 Lord.
All you hosts of the Lord, bless the Lord.
Sun and moon, bless the Lord.
Stars of heaven, bless the Lord.

Every shower and dew, bless the Lord.
All you winds, bless the Lord.
Fire and heat, bless the Lord.
Cold and chill, bless the Lord.—

Dew and rain, bless the Lord.
Frost and chill, bless the Lord.
Ice and snow, bless the Lord.
Nights and days, bless the Lord.
Light and darkness, bless the Lord.
Lightnings and clouds, bless the Lord.

Let the earth bless the Lord.
Praise and exalt him above all forever.
Mountains and hills, bless the Lord.
Everything growing from the earth, bless the
 Lord.
You springs, bless the Lord.
Seas and rivers, bless the Lord.
You dolphins and all water creatures, bless the
 Lord.
All you birds of the air, bless the Lord.

All you beasts, wild and tame, bless the Lord.
You sons of men, bless the Lord.

O Israel, bless the Lord.
Praise and exalt him above all forever.
Priests of the Lord, bless the Lord.
Servants of the Lord, bless the Lord.
Spirits and souls of the just, bless the Lord.
Holy men of humble heart, bless the Lord.
Hananiah, Azariah, Mishael, bless the Lord.
Praise and exalt him above all forever.

Let us bless the Father, and the Son, and the
    Holy Spirit.
Let us praise and exalt him above all forever.
Blessed are you, Lord, in the firmament of
    heaven.
Praiseworthy and glorious and exalted above
    all forever.

Ant. 3   A little child is born for us today; little
             and yet called the mighty God, alleluia.

Psalm 149
The joy of God's holy people

*Let the sons of the Church, the children of the
new people, rejoice in Christ, their King* (Hesychius).

Sing a new song to the Lord,
his praise in the assembly of the faithful.

Let Israel rejoice in its Maker,
let Zion's sons exult in their king.
Let them praise his name with dancing
and make music with timbrel and harp.

For the Lord takes delight in his people.
He crowns the poor with salvation.
Let the faithful rejoice in their glory,
shout for joy and take their rest.
Let the praise of God be on their lips
and a two-edged sword in their hand,

to deal out vengeance to the nations
and punishment on all the peoples;
to bind their kings in chains
and their nobles in fetters of iron;
to carry out the sentence pre-ordained:
this honor is for all his faithful.

Psalm-prayer

Let Israel rejoice in you, Lord, and acknowledge you as creator and redeemer. We put our trust in your faithfulness and proclaim the wonderful truths of salvation. May your loving kindness embrace us now and for ever.

READING   *Hebrews 1:1-4*

In times past, God spoke in fragmentary and varied ways to our fathers through the prophets; in this, the final age, he has spoken to us through his Son, whom he has made heir of all things and through whom he first created the universe. This Son is the reflection of the Father's glory, the exact representation of the Father's being, and he sustains all things by his powerful word. When he had cleansed us from our sins, he took his seat at the right hand of the Majesty in heaven, as far superior to the angels as the name he has inherited is superior to theirs.

RESPONSORY

The Lord has made known, alleluia, alleluia.
—The Lord has made known, alleluia, alleluia.

His saving power.
—Alleluia, alleluia.

Glory to the Father . . .
—The Lord has . . .

CANTICLE OF ZECHARIAH

Ant. Glory to God in the highest, and peace to his people on earth, alleluia.

INTERCESSIONS

The Word of God existed before the creation of the universe yet was born among us in time.

We praise and worship him as we cry out in
joy:
*Let the earth ring out with joy for you have
come.*

You are the eternal Word of God who flooded
the world with joy at your birth,
—fill us with joy by the continuous gift of your
life.

You saved us and by your birth revealed to us
the covenant faithfulness of the Lord,
—help us to be faithful to the promises of our
baptism.
You are the King of heaven and earth who sent
messengers to announce peace to all,
—let our lives be filled with your peace.
You are the true vine that brings forth the fruit
of life,
—make us branches of the vine, bearing much
fruit.

Our Father . . .

PRAYER

Father,
we are filled with the new light
by the coming of your Word among us.

May the light of faith
shine in our words and actions.

Grant this through our Lord Jesus Christ, your
    Son,
who lives and reigns with you and the Holy
    Spirit,
one God, for ever and ever.

May the Lord bless us,
protect us from all evil
and bring us to everlasting life.
—Amen.

EVENING PRAYER

God, come to my assistance.
—Lord, make haste to help me.

Glory to the Father, and to the Son, and to the
   Holy Spirit:
as it was in the beginning, is now, and will be
   for ever. Amen. Alleluia.

Ant. 1   You have been endowed from your birth
         with princely gifts; in eternal splendor,
         before the dawn of light on earth, I have
         begotten you.

Psalm 110:1–5, 7

The Lord's revelation to my Master:
"Sit on my right:
your foes I will put beneath your feet."

The Lord will wield from Zion
your scepter of power:
rule in the midst of all your foes.

A prince from the day of your birth
on the holy mountains;
from the womb before the dawn I begot you.

The Lord has sworn an oath he will not
   change.

"You are a priest for ever,
a priest like Melchizedek of old!"

The Master standing at your right hand
will shatter kings in the day of his great wrath.
He shall drink from the stream by the wayside
and therefore he shall lift up his head.

Ant. 2   With the Lord is unfailing love; great is
           his power to save.

Psalm 130

Out of the depths I cry to you, O Lord,
Lord, hear my voice!
O let your ears be attentive
to the voice of my pleading.

If you, O Lord, should mark our guilt,
Lord, who would survive?
But with you is found forgiveness:
for this we revere you.

My soul is waiting for the Lord,
I count on his word.
My soul is longing for the Lord
more than watchman for daybreak.
Let the watchman count on daybreak
and Israel on the Lord.

Because with the Lord there is mercy
and fullness of redemption,

Israel indeed he will redeem
from all its iniquity.

Ant. 3 In the beginning, before time began, the
Word was God; today he is born, the Savior of the world.

CANTICLE *Colossians 1:12–20*

Let us give thanks to the Father
for having made you worthy
to share the lot of the saints
in light.

He rescued us
from the power of darkness
and brought us
into the kingdom of his beloved Son.
Through him we have redemption,
the forgiveness of our sins.

He is the image of the invisible God,
the first-born of all creatures.
In him everything in heaven and on earth was
    created,
things visible and invisible.

All were created through him;
all were created for him.
He is before all else that is.
In him everything continues in being.

It is he who is head of the body, the church;
he who is the beginning,
the first-born of the dead,
so that primacy may be his in everything.

It pleased God to make absolute fullness reside
  in him
and, by means of him, to reconcile everything
  in his person,
both on earth and in the heavens,
making peace through the blood of his cross.

READING   *1 John 1:1–3*

This is what we proclaim to you:
what was from the beginning,
what we have heard,
what we have seen with our eyes,
what we have looked upon
and our hands have touched—
we speak of the word of life.
(This life became visible;
we have seen and bear witness to it,
and we proclaim to you the eternal life
that was present to the Father
and became visible to us.)
What we have seen and heard
we proclaim in turn to you
so that you may share life with us.

This fellowship of ours is with the Father
and with his Son, Jesus Christ.

RESPONSORY

The Word was made man, alleluia, alleluia.
—The Word was made man, alleluia, alleluia.

He lived among us.
—Alleluia, alleluia.

Glory to the Father . . .
—The Word was . . .

CANTICLE OF MARY

Ant.   Christ the Lord is born today; today, the
Savior has appeared. Earth echoes songs
of angel choirs, archangels' joyful praise.
Today on earth his friends exult: Glory to
God in the highest, alleluia.

INTERCESSIONS

At the birth of Jesus, angels proclaimed
peace to the world. We worship him now
with joy, and we pray with hearts full of
faith:
May your birth bring peace to all.
Lord, fill your holy people with whatever good
they need,

—let the mystery of your birth be the source of
   our peace.
You came as chief shepherd and guardian of
   our lives,
—let the pope and bishops be faithful chan-
   nels of your many gifts of grace.
King from all eternity, you desired to be born
   within time and to experience the day-to-
   day life of men and women,
—share your gift of unending life with us,
   weak people, doomed to death.
Awaited from the beginning of the world, you
   came only in the fullness of time,
—now reveal your presence to those who are
   still expecting you.
You became man and gave new life to our
   human condition in the grip of death,
—now give the fullness of life to all who have
   died.

Our Father . . .

PRAYER

Lord God,
we praise you for creating man,
and still more for restoring him in Christ.
Your Son shared our weakness:
may we share his glory,

for he lives and reigns with you and the Holy
   Spirit,
one God, for ever and ever.

May the Lord bless us,
protect us from all evil
and bring us to everlasting life.
—Amen.

Lenten Season

*. . . may our repentence bring us
the blessing of God's forgiveness . . .*

THIS SECTION MAY BE PRAYED
FROM ASH WEDNESDAY
TO THE VIGIL OF EASTER

MORNING PRAYER

God, come to my assistance.
—Lord, make haste to help me.

Glory to the Father, and to the Son, and to the
   Holy Spirit:
as it was in the beginning, is now, and will be
   for ever. Amen.

PSALMODY

Ant. 1 O God, my God, I give you thanks; you are
       my God, I shall proclaim your glory.

Psalm 118
Song of joy for salvation

*This Jesus is the stone which, rejected by you
builders, has become the chief stone supporting
all the rest* (Acts 4:11).

Give thanks to the Lord for he is good,
for his love endures for ever.

Let the sons of Israel say:
"His love endures for ever."
Let the sons of Aaron say:
"His love endures for ever."
Let those who fear the Lord say:
"His love endures for ever."

I called to the Lord in my distress;
he answered and freed me.
The Lord is at my side; I do not fear.
What can man do against me?
The Lord is at my side as my helper:
I shall look down on my foes.

It is better to take refuge in the Lord
than to trust in men:
it is better to take refuge in the Lord
than to trust in princes.

The nations all encompassed me;
in the Lord's name I crushed them.
They compassed me, compassed me about;
in the Lord's name I crushed them.
They compassed me about like bees;
they blazed like a fire among thorns.
In the Lord's name I crushed them.

I was hard-pressed and was falling
but the Lord came to help me.
The Lord is my strength and my song;
he is my savior.

There are shouts of joy and victory
in the tents of the just.

The Lord's right hand has triumphed;
his right hand raised me.

The Lord's right hand has triumphed;
I shall not die, I shall live
and recount his deeds.
I was punished, I was punished by the Lord,
but not doomed to die.

Open to me the gates of holiness:
I will enter and give thanks.
This is the Lord's own gate
where the just may enter.
I will thank you for you have answered
and you are my savior.

The stone which the builders rejected
has become the corner stone.
This is the work of the Lord,
a marvel in our eyes.
This day was made by the Lord;
we rejoice and are glad.

O Lord, grant us salvation;
O Lord, grant success.
Blessed in the name of the Lord
is he who comes.
We bless you from the house of the Lord;
the Lord God is our light.

Go forward in procession with branches
even to the altar.
You are my God, I thank you.

My God, I praise you.
Give thanks to the Lord for he is good;
for his love endures for ever.

Psalm-prayer

Lord God, you have given us the great day of
rejoicing: Jesus Christ, the stone rejected by the
builders, has become the cornerstone of the
Church, our spiritual home. Shed upon your
Church the rays of your glory, that it may be seen
as the gate of salvation open to all nations. Let
cries of joy and exultation ring out from its
tents, to celebrate the wonder of Christ's resurrection.

Ant. 2   God of might, deliver us; free us from the
power of the enemy.

CANTICLE   *Daniel 3:52–57*
Let all creatures praise the Lord

The Creator . . . is blessed for ever (Romans 1:25).

Blessed are you, O Lord, the God of our fathers,
praiseworthy and exalted above all forever.

And blessed is your holy and glorious name,
praiseworthy and exalted above all for all
ages.

Blessed are you in the temple of your holy
glory,

praiseworthy and glorious above all forever.

Blessed are you on the throne of your kingdom,
praiseworthy and exalted above all forever.

Blessed are you who look into the depths
from your throne upon the cherubim,
praiseworthy and exalted above all forever.

Blessed are you in the firmament of heaven,
praiseworthy and glorious forever.

Bless the Lord, all you works of the Lord,
praise and exalt him above all forever.

Ant. 3   Praise God for his mighty deeds.

Psalm 150
Praise the Lord

*Let mind and heart be in your song: this is to
glorify God with your whole self* (Hesychius).

Praise God in his holy place,
praise him in his mighty heavens.
Praise him for his powerful deeds,
praise his surpassing greatness.

O praise him with sound of trumpet,
praise him with lute and harp.
Praise him with timbrel and dance,
praise him with strings and pipes.

O praise him with resounding cymbals,
praise him with clashing of cymbals.
Let everything that lives and that breathes
give praise to the Lord.

Psalm-prayer

Lord God, maker of heaven and earth and of
all created things, you make your just ones holy
and you justify sinners who confess your name.
Hear us as we humbly pray to you: give us eternal joy with your saints.

READING   *Nehemiah 8:9, 10*

Today is holy to the Lord your God. Do not be
sad, and do not weep; for today is holy to our
Lord. Do not be saddened this day, for rejoicing
in the Lord must be your strength!

RESPONSORY

Christ, Son of the living God, have mercy on
   us.
—Christ, Son of the living God, have mercy on
   us.

You were wounded for our offenses,
—have mercy on us.

Glory to the Father . . .
—Christ, Son of the living God, have mercy on
   us.

CANTICLE OF ZECHARIAH

Ant. It was unheard of for anyone to open the
eyes of a man born blind until the coming
of Christ, the Son of God.

INTERCESSIONS

Let us give glory to God, whose kindness knows
no limit.
Through Jesus Christ, who lives for ever to
intercede for us, let us pray:
Kindle in our hearts the fire of your love.
God of mercy, let today be a day rich in good
works,
—a day of generosity to all we meet.
From the waters of the flood you saved Noah
through the ark,
—from the waters of baptism raise up to new
life those under instruction.
May we live not by bread only,
—but by every word falling from your lips.
Help us to do away with all dissension,
—so that we may rejoice in your gifts of peace
and love.

Our Father . . .

Prayer

Father of peace,
we are joyful in your Word,

your Son Jesus Christ,
who reconciles us to you.
Let us hasten toward Easter
with the eagerness of faith and love.

We ask this through our Lord Jesus Christ,
   your Son
who lives and reigns with you and the Holy
   Spirit,
one God, for ever and ever.

May the Lord bless us,
protect us from all evil
and bring us to everlasting life.
—Amen.

EVENING PRAYER

God, come to my assistance.
—Lord, make haste to help me.

Glory to the Father, and to the Son, and to the
Holy Spirit:
as it was in the beginning, is now, and will be
for ever. Amen.

Ant. 1   God has appointed Christ to be judge of
the living and the dead.

Psalm 110:1–5, 7
The Messiah, king and priest

*Christ's reign will last until all his enemies are
made subject to him* (1 Corinthians 15:25).

The Lord's revelation to my Master:
"Sit on my right:
your foes I will put beneath your feet."

The Lord will wield from Zion
your scepter of power:
rule in the midst of all your foes.

A prince from the day of your birth
on the holy mountains;
from the womb before the dawn I begot you.

The Lord has sworn an oath he will not
   change.
"You are a priest for ever,
a priest like Melchizedek of old."

The Master standing at your right hand
will shatter kings in the day of his great wrath.

He shall drink from the stream by the wayside
and therefore he shall lift up his head.

Psalm-prayer

Father, we ask you to give us victory and
peace. In Jesus Christ, our Lord and King, we are
already seated at your right hand. We look forward to praising you in the fellowship of all your
saints in our heavenly homeland.

Ant. 2   Happy the man who shows mercy for the
          Lord's sake; he will stand firm for ever.

Psalm 112
The happiness of the just man

*Live as children born of the light. Light produces
every kind of goodness and justice and truth*
(Ephesians 5:8–9).

Happy the man who fears the Lord,
who takes delight in all his commands.
His sons will be powerful on earth;
the children of the upright are blessed.

Riches and wealth are in his house;
his justice stands firm for ever.
He is light in the darkness for the upright:
he is generous, merciful and just.

The good man takes pity and lends,
he conducts his affairs with honor.
The just man will never waver:
he will be remembered for ever.

He has no fear of evil news;
with a firm heart he trusts in the Lord.
With a steadfast heart he will not fear;
he will see the downfall of his foes.

Open-handed, he gives to the poor;
his justice stands firm for ever.
His head will be raised in glory.

The wicked man sees and is angry,
grinds his teeth and fades away;
the desire of the wicked leads to doom.

Psalm-prayer

Lord God, you are the eternal light which illumines the hearts of good people. Help us to love you, to rejoice in your glory, and so to live in this world as to avoid harsh judgment in the next. May we come to see the light of your countenance.

Ant. 3 **Those things, which God foretold through his prophets concerning the suffering that Christ would endure, have been fulfilled.**

CANTICLE   *1 Peter 2:21–24*
The willing acceptance of his passion by
Christ, the servant of God

Christ suffered for you,
and left you an example
to have you follow in his footsteps.

He did no wrong;
no deceit was found in his mouth.
When he was insulted,
he returned no insult.

When he was made to suffer,
he did not counter with threats.
Instead he delivered himself up
to the One who judges justly.

In his own body
he brought your sins to the cross,
so that all of us, dead to sin,
could live in accord with God's will.

By his wounds you were healed.

READING   *1 Corinthians 9:24–27*

While all the runners in the stadium take part in the race, the award goes to one man. In that case, run so as to win! Athletes deny themselves all sorts of things. They do this to win a crown of leaves that withers, but we a crown that is imperishable. I do not run like a man who loses sight of the finish line. I do not fight as if I were shadowboxing. What I do is discipline my own body and master it, for fear that after having preached to others I myself should be rejected.

RESPONSORY

Listen to us, O Lord, and have mercy, for we have sinned against you.
—Listen to us, O Lord, and have mercy, for we have sinned against you.

Christ Jesus, hear our humble petitions,
—for we have sinned against you.

Glory to the Father . . .
—Listen to us . . .

CANTICLE OF MARY

Ant.   My son, you have been with me all the time and everything I have is yours. But we had to feast and rejoice, because your brother was dead and has come to life again; he was lost to us and now has been found.

INTERCESSIONS

Let us give thanks continually to Christ, our teacher and our head, who came to serve and to do good to all.
In humility and confidence let us ask him:
Come, Lord, to visit your family.

Lord, be present to the bishops and priests of your Church, who share your role as head and shepherd,
—may they lead your people to the Father under your guidance.

May your angel be with all who travel,
—to keep them safe in soul and body.

Teach us to serve the needs of others,
—and to be like you, who came to serve, not to be served.

Grant that in the human family, brother may always help brother,
—so that, with your assistance, it may be a city compact and strong.

Have mercy on all the departed,
—bring them to the vision of your glory.

Our Father . . .

PRAYER

Father of peace,
we are joyful in your Word,
your Son Jesus Christ,
who reconciles us to you.
Let us hasten toward Easter
with the eagerness of faith and love.

We ask this through our Lord Jesus Christ,
    your Son,
who lives and reigns with you and the Holy
    Spirit, one God, for ever and ever.

May the Lord bless us,
protect us from all evil
and bring us to everlasting life.
—Amen.

MORNING PRAYER

God, come to my assistance.
—Lord, make haste to help me.

Glory to the Father, and to the Son, and to the
   Holy Spirit:
as it was in the beginning, is now, and will be
   for ever. Amen.

Ant. 1 When will I come to the end of my pil-
        grimage and enter the presence of God?

Psalm 42
Longing for the Lord's presence in his Temple
*Let all who thirst come; let all who desire it
drink from the life-giving water* (Revelation 22:
17).

Like the deer that yearns
for running streams,
so my soul is yearning
for you, my God.

My soul is thirsting for God,
the God of my life;
when can I enter and see
the face of God?

My tears have become my bread,
by night, by day,
as I hear it said all the day long:
"Where is your God?"

These things will I remember
as I pour out my soul:
how I would lead the rejoicing crowd
into the house of God,
amid cries of gladness and thanksgiving,
the throng wild with joy.

Why are you cast down, my soul,
why groan within me?
Hope in God; I will praise him still,
my savior and my God.

My soul is cast down within me
as I think of you,
from the country of Jordan and Mount Her-
    mon,
from the Hill of Mizar.

Deep is calling on deep,
in the roar of waters:
your torrents and all your waves
swept over me.

By day the Lord will send
his loving kindness;

by night I will sing to him,
praise the God of my life.

I will say to God, my rock:
"Why have you forgotten me?
Why do I go mourning,
oppressed by the foe?"

With cries that pierce me to the heart,
my enemies revile me,
saying to me all the day long:
"Where is your God?"

Why are you cast down, my soul,
why groan within me?
Hope in God; I will praise him still,
my savior and my God.

Psalm-prayer

Father in heaven, when your strength takes possession of us we no longer say: Why are you cast down, my soul? So now that the surging waves of our indignation have passed over us, let us feel the healing calm of your forgiveness. Inspire us to yearn for you always, like the deer for running streams, until you satisfy every longing in heaven.

Ant. 2   Lord, show us the radiance of your
         mercy.

CANTICLE   *Sirach 36:1–5, 10–13*
Prayer of entreaty for the holy city, Jerusalem

This is eternal life: to know you, the one true
God, and Jesus Christ whom you have sent
(John 17:3).

Come to our aid, O God of the universe,
and put all the nations in dread of you!
Raise your hand against the heathen,
that they may realize your power.

As you have used us to show them your holi-
    ness,
so now use them to show us your glory.
Thus they will know, as you know,
that there is no God but you.

Give new signs and work new wonders;
show forth the splendor of your right hand and
    arm.

Gather all the tribes of Jacob,
that they may inherit the land as of old.
Show mercy to the people called by your name;
Israel, whom you named your first-born.

Take pity on your holy city,
Jerusalem, your dwelling place.
Fill Zion with your majesty,
your temple with your glory.

Ant. 3 **The vaults of heaven ring with your praise, O God**

Psalm 19A
Praise of the Lord, Creator of all

The dawn from on high shall break on us . . . to guide our feet into the way of peace (Luke 1:78, 79).

The heavens proclaim the glory of God
and the firmament shows forth the work of his hands.
Day unto day takes up the story
and night unto night makes known the message.

No speech, no word, no voice is heard
yet their span extends through all the earth,
their words to the utmost bounds of the world.

There he has placed a tent for the sun;
it comes forth like a bridegroom coming from his tent,
rejoices like a champion to run its course.

At the end of the sky is the rising of the sun;
to the furthest end of the sky is its course.
There is nothing concealed from its burning heat.

Psalm-prayer

To enlighten the world, Father, you sent to us
your Word as the sun of truth and justice shining
upon mankind. Illumine our eyes that we may
discern your glory in the many works of your
hand.

READING   *Exodus 19:4–6a*

You have seen for yourselves how I bore you
up on eagle wings and brought you here to myself. Therefore if you hearken to my voice and
keep my covenant, you shall be my special possession, dearer to me than all other people,
though all the earth is mine. You shall be a kingdom of priests, a holy nation.

RESPONSORY

God himself will set me free, from the hunter's
    snare.
—God himself will set me free, from the
    hunter's snare.

From those who would trap me with lying
    words
—and from the hunter's snare.

Glory to the Father . . .
—God himself will . . .

CANTICLE OF ZECHARIAH

Ant.   Be compassionate and forgiving as your
       Father is, says the Lord.

INTERCESSIONS

Blessed be God the Father for his gift of this
   sacrifice of praise. In the spirit of this Lenten
   season, let us pray:
   *Instruct us, Lord, in the ways of your king-
   dom.*
God of power and mercy, give us the spirit of
   prayer and repentance,
—with burning love for you and for all mankind.
Help us to work with you in making all things
   new in Christ,
—and in spreading justice and peace throughout the world.

Teach us the meaning and value of creation,
—so that we may join its voice to ours as we
   sing your praise.
Forgive us for failing to see Christ in the poor,
   the distressed and the troublesome,
—and for our failure to reverence your Son in
   their persons.

Our Father . . .

PRAYER

God our Father,
teach us to find new life through penance.
Keep us from sin,
and help us live by your commandment of
    love.

We ask this through our Lord Jesus Christ,
    your Son,
who lives and reigns with you and the Holy
    Spirit,
one God, for ever and ever.

May the Lord bless us,
protect us from all evil
and bring us to everlasting life.
—Amen.

EVENING PRAYER

God, come to my assistance.
—Lord, make haste to help me.

Glory to the Father, and to the Son, and to the
  Holy Spirit:
as it was in the beginning, is now, and will be
  for ever. Amen.

PSALMODY

Ant. 1   Yours is more than mortal beauty; every
          word you speak is full of grace.

Psalm 45
The marriage of the king
The Bridegroom is here; go out and welcome him
(Matthew 25:6).

I

My heart overflows with noble words.
To the king I must speak the song I have made;
my tongue as nimble as the pen of a scribe.

You are the fairest of the children of men
and graciousness is poured upon your lips:
because God has blessed you for evermore.

O mighty one, gird your sword upon your
  thigh;
in splendor and state, ride on in triumph

for the cause of truth and goodness and
    right.

Take aim with your bow in your dread right
    hand.
Your arrows are sharp: peoples fall beneath
    you.
The foes of the king fall down and lose heart.

Your throne, O God, shall endure for ever.
A scepter of justice is the scepter of your king-
    dom.
Your love is for justice; your hatred for evil.

Therefore God, your God, has anointed you
with the oil of gladness above other kings:
your robes are fragrant with aloes and myrrh.

From the ivory palace you are greeted with
    music.
The daughters of kings are among your loved
    ones.
On your right stands the queen in gold of
    Ophir.

Ant. 2   The Bridegroom is here; go out and wel-
       come him.

II

Listen, O daughter, give ear to my words:
forget your own people and your father's house.

So will the king desire your beauty:
he is your lord, pay homage to him.

And the people of Tyre shall come with gifts,
the richest of the people shall seek your
favor.
The daughter of the king is clothed with splendor,
her robes embroidered with pearls set in
gold.

She is led to the king with her maiden companions.
They are escorted amid gladness and joy;
they pass within the palace of the king.

Sons shall be yours in place of your fathers:
you will make them princes over all the earth.
May this song make your name for ever
remembered.
May the peoples praise you from age to age.

Psalm-prayer

When you took on flesh, Lord Jesus, you made
a marriage of mankind with God. Help us to be
faithful to your word and endure our exile
bravely, until we are called to the heavenly marriage feast, to which the Virgin Mary, exemplar
of your Church, has preceded us.

Ant. 3 **God planned in the fullness of time to
        restore all things in Christ**

CANTICLE   *Ephesians 1:3–10*
                God our Savior

Praised be the God and Father
of our Lord Jesus Christ
who has bestowed on us in Christ
every spiritual blessing in the heavens.

God chose us in him
before the world began
to be holy
and blameless in his sight.

He predestined us
to be adopted sons through Jesus Christ,
such was his will and pleasure,
that all might praise the glorious favor
he has bestowed on us in his beloved.

In him and through his blood, we have been
    redeemed,
and our sins forgiven,
so immeasurably generous
is God's favor to us.

God has given us the wisdom
to understand fully the mystery,

the plan he was pleased
to decree in Christ.

A plan to be carried out
in Christ, in the fullness of time,
to bring all things into one in him,
in the heavens and on earth.

READING ——————————————— *Romans 12:1–2*

Brothers, I beg you through the mercy of God
to offer your bodies as a living sacrifice holy and
acceptable to God, your spiritual worship. Do not
conform yourselves to this age but be transformed by the renewal of your mind, so that you
may judge what is God's will, what is good,
pleasing and perfect.

RESPONSORY

To you, O Lord, I make my prayer for
    mercy.
—To you, O Lord, I make my prayer for
    mercy.

Heal my soul, for I have sinned against you.
—I make my prayer for mercy.

Glory to the Father . . .
—To you, O Lord . . .

CANTICLE OF MARY

Ant.   Do not judge others, and you will not be
        judged, for as you have judged them, so
        God will judge you.

INTERCESSIONS

Glory to God the Father, who has promised
    through his Son to grant what is asked by
    those who pray together. With confidence in
    this promise, let us pray:
    Lord, look with favor on your people.
Lord, you gave the Law to Moses on Mount
    Sinai, and brought it to perfection in your
    anointed one,
—may all recognize the Law written in their
    hearts, and keep it faithfully as a covenant.
Give those in authority a true concern for their
    brothers and sisters entrusted to their care,
—and inspire the hearts of the people to sup-
    port their leaders.
Strengthen with your Spirit the minds and
    hearts of missionaries,
—and raise up a great company to help them
    from every nation.

Give your grace to children, that they may
    grow in your favor,
—and to young people, that they may reach

their full stature by loving you and keeping your commandments.

Our Father . . .

PRAYER

God our Father,
teach us to find new life through penance.
Keep us from sin,
and help us live by your commandment of
    love.

We ask this through our Lord Jesus Christ,
    your Son,
who lives and reigns with you and the Holy
    Spirit,
one God, for ever and ever.

May the Lord bless us,
protect us from all evil
and bring us to everlasting life.
—Amen.

MORNING PRAYER

God, come to my assistance.
—Lord, make haste to help me.

Glory to the Father, and to the Son, and to the
   Holy Spirit:
as it was in the beginning, is now, and will be
   for ever. Amen.

PSALMODY

Ant. 1   A humble, contrite heart, O God, you will
          not spurn.

Psalm 51
O God, have mercy on me

*Your inmost being must be renewed, and you
must put on the new man* (Ephesians 4:23–24).

Have mercy on me, God, in your kindness.
In your compassion blot out my offense.
O wash me more and more from my guilt
and cleanse me from my sin.

My offenses truly I know them;
my sin is always before me.
Against you, you alone, have I sinned;
what is evil in your sight I have done.

That you may be justified when you give sentence

and be without reproach when you judge.—
O see, in guilt I was born,
a sinner was I conceived.

Indeed you love truth in the heart;
then in the secret of my heart teach me wis-
    dom.
O purify me, then I shall be clean;
O wash me, I shall be whiter than snow.

Make me hear rejoicing and gladness,
that the bones you have crushed may revive.
From my sins turn away your face
and blot out all my guilt.

A pure heart create for me, O God,
put a steadfast spirit within me.
Do not cast me away from your presence,
nor deprive me of your holy spirit.

Give me again the joy of your help;
with a spirit of fervor sustain me,
that I may teach transgressors your ways
and sinners may return to you.

O rescue me, God, my helper,
and my tongue shall ring out your goodness.
O Lord, open my lips
and my mouth shall declare your praise.

For in sacrifice you take no delight,
burnt offering from me you would refuse,

my sacrifice, a contrite spirit.
A humbled, contrite heart you will not spurn.

In your goodness, show favor to Zion:
rebuild the walls of Jerusalem.
Then you will be pleased with lawful sacrifice,
holocausts offered on your altar.

Psalm-prayer

Father, he who knew no sin was made sin for
us, to save us and restore us to your friendship.
Look upon our contrite heart and afflicted spirit
and heal our troubled conscience, so that in the
joy and strength of the Holy Spirit we may proclaim your praise and glory before all the nations.

Ant. 2   Even in your anger, Lord, you will re-
         member compassion.

CANTICLE   *Habakkuk 3:2–4, 13a, 15–19*
                 God comes to judge

*Lift up your heads for your redemption is at
hand* (Luke 21:28).

O Lord, I have heard your renown,
and feared, O Lord, your work.
In the course of the years revive it,
in the course of the years make it known;
in your wrath remember compassion!

God comes from Teman,
the Holy One from Mount Paran.
Covered are the heavens with his glory,
and with his praise the earth is filled.

His splendor spreads like the light;
rays shine forth from beside him,
where his power is concealed.
You come forth to save your people,
to save your anointed one.

You tread the sea with your steeds
amid the churning of the deep waters.
I hear, and my body trembles;
at the sound, my lips quiver.

Decay invades my bones,
my legs tremble beneath me.
I await the day of distress
that will come upon the people who attack us.

For though the fig tree blossom not
nor fruit be on the vines,
though the yield of the olive fail
and the terraces produce no nourishment,

Though the flocks disappear from the fold
and there be no herd in the stalls,
yet will I rejoice in the Lord
and exult in my saving God.

God, my Lord, is my strength;
he makes my feet swift as those of hinds
and enables me to go upon the heights.

Ant. 3 O praise the Lord, Jerusalem!

Psalm 147: 12–20
The restoration of Jerusalem

Come, I will show you the bride of the Lamb
(Revelation 21:9).

O praise the Lord, Jerusalem!
Zion, praise your God!

He has strengthened the bars of your gates,
he has blessed the children within you.
He established peace on your borders,
he feeds you with finest wheat.

He sends out his word to the earth
and swiftly runs his command.
He showers down snow white as wool,
he scatters hoar-frost like ashes.

He hurls down hailstones like crumbs.
The waters are frozen at his touch;
he sends forth his word and it melts them:
at the breath of his mouth the waters flow.

He makes his word known to Jacob,
to Israel his laws and decrees.—

He has not dealt thus with other nations;
he has not taught them his decrees.

Psalm-prayer

Lord, you established peace within the borders
of Jerusalem. Give the fullness of peace now to
your faithful people. May peace rule us in this
life and possess us in eternal life. You are about
to fill us with the best of wheat; grant that what
we see dimly now as in a mirror, we may come
to perceive clearly in the brightness of your
truth.

READING   *James 5:16, 19–20*

Declare your sins to one another, and pray for
one another, that you may find healing. The fer-
vent petition of a holy man is powerful indeed.
My brothers, the case may arise among you of
someone straying from the truth, and of another
bringing him back. Remember this: the person
who brings a sinner back from his way will save
his soul from death and cancel a multitude of
sins.

RESPONSORY

To you, O Lord, I make my prayer for mercy.
—To you, O Lord, I make my prayer for mercy.

Heal my soul, for I have sinned against you.
—I make my prayer for mercy.

Glory to the Father . . .
—To you, O Lord . . .

CANTICLE OF ZECHARIAH

Ant. They would have arrested Jesus but they feared the people who regarded him as a prophet.

INTERCESSIONS

The Savior of mankind by dying destroyed death and by rising again restored life. Let us humbly ask him:
Sanctify your people, redeemed by your blood.
Redeemer of the world, give us a greater share of your passion through a deeper spirit of repentance,
—so that we may share the glory of your resurrection.
May your Mother, comfort of the afflicted, protect us,
—may we console others as you console us.
In their trials enable your faithful people to share in your passion,

—and so reveal in their lives your saving
    power.
You humbled yourself by being obedient even
    to accepting death, death on a cross,
—give all who serve you the gifts of obedience
    and patient endurance.
Transform the bodies of the dead to be like
    your own in glory,
—and bring us at last into their fellowship.

Our Father . . .

PRAYER

Merciful Father,
may our acts of penance bring us your forgive-
    ness,
open our hearts to your love,
and prepare us for the coming feast of the res-
    urrection.

We ask this through our Lord Jesus Christ,
    your Son,
who lives and reigns with you and the Holy
    Spirit,
one God, for ever and ever.

May the Lord bless us,
protect us from all evil
and bring us to everlasting life.
—Amen.

EVENING PRAYER

God, come to my assistance.
—Lord, make haste to help me.

Glory to the Father, and to the Son, and to the
Holy Spirit:
as it was in the beginning, is now, and will be
for ever. Amen.

PSALMODY

Ant. 1   Lord, keep my soul from death, never let
me stumble.

Psalm 116: 1–9
Thanksgiving

*We must endure many trials before entering
God's kingdom* (Acts 14:21).

I love the Lord for he has heard
the cry of my appeal;
for he turned his ear to me
in the day when I called him.

They surrounded me, the snares of death,
with the anguish of the tomb;
they caught me, sorrow and distress.
I called on the Lord's name.

O Lord my God, deliver me!

How gracious is the Lord, and just;
our God has compassion.
The Lord protects the simple hearts;
I was helpless so he saved me.

Turn back, my soul, to your rest
for the Lord has been good;
he has kept my soul from death,
my eyes from tears
and my feet from stumbling.

I will walk in the presence of the Lord
in the land of the living.

Psalm-prayer

God of power and mercy, through your Son's
passion and resurrection you have freed us from
the bonds of death and the anguish of separation
from you. Be ever with us on our pilgrimage;
then we shall sing rather than weep. Keep our
feet from stumbling so that we may be able to
follow you until we come to eternal rest.

Ant. 2   My help comes from the Lord, who made
heaven and earth.

Psalm 121
Guardian of his people

*Never again will they hunger and thirst, never
again know scorching heat* (Revelation 7:16).

I lift up my eyes to the mountains:
from where shall come my help?
My help shall come from the Lord
who made heaven and earth.

May he never allow you to stumble!
Let him sleep not, your guard.
No, he sleeps not nor slumbers,
Israel's guard.

The Lord is your guard and your shade;
at your right side he stands.
By day the sun shall not smite you
nor the moon in the night.

The Lord will guard you from evil,
he will guard your soul.
The Lord will guard your going and coming
both now and for ever.

Psalm-prayer

Lord Jesus Christ, you have prepared a quiet
place for us in your Father's eternal home.
Watch over our welfare on this perilous journey,
shade us from the burning heat of day, and keep
our lives free of evil until the end.

Ant. 3 King of all the ages, your ways are perfect and true.

CANTICLE   *Revelation 15:3–4*
Hymn of adoration

Mighty and wonderful are your works,
Lord God Almighty!
Righteous and true are your ways,
O King of the nations!

Who would dare refuse you honor,
or the glory due your name, O Lord?

Since you alone are holy,
all nations shall come
and worship in your presence.
Your mighty deeds are clearly seen.

READING   *James 5:16, 19–20*

Declare your sins to one another, and pray for
one another, that you may find healing. The fer-
vent petition of a holy man is powerful indeed.
My brothers, the case may arise among you of
someone straying from the truth, and of another
bringing him back. Remember this: the person
who brings a sinner back from his way will save
his soul from death and cancel a multitude of
sins.

RESPONSORY

To you, O Lord, I make my prayer for mercy.
—To you, O Lord, I make my prayer for mercy.

Heal my soul, for I have sinned against you.
—I make my prayer for mercy.

Glory to the Father . . .
—To you, O Lord . . .

CANTICLE OF MARY

Ant. They would have arrested Jesus but they
feared the people who regarded him as a
prophet.

INTERCESSIONS

The Savior of mankind by dying destroyed
death and by rising again restored life. Let
us humbly ask him:
*Sanctify your people, redeemed by your
blood.*

Redeemer of the world, give us a greater share
of your passion through a deeper spirit of
repentance,
—so that we may share the glory of your resurrection.
May your Mother, comfort of the afflicted, protect us,
—may we console others as you console us.
Look with love on those who suffer because of
our indifference,
—come to their aid, and turn our uncaring

hearts to works of justice and charity.

You humbled yourself by being obedient even
to accepting death, death on a cross,

—give all who serve you the gifts of obedience
and patient endurance.

Transform the bodies of the dead to be like
your own in glory,

—and bring us at last into their fellowship.

Our Father . . .

PRAYER

Merciful Father,

may our acts of penance bring us your forgiveness,

open our hearts to your love,

and prepare us for the coming feast of the resurrection.

We ask this through our Lord Jesus Christ,
your Son,

who lives and reigns with you and the Holy
Spirit,

one God, for ever and ever.

May the Lord bless us,

protect us from all evil

and bring us to everlasting life.

—Amen.

Easter Season

*. . . may we follow Him
in His risen life . . .*

THIS SECTION MAY BE PRAYED FROM EASTER
TO THE FEAST OF PENTECOST

Morning Prayer

God, come to my assistance.
—Lord, make haste to help me.

Glory to the Father, and to the Son, and to the
    Holy Spirit:
as it was in the beginning, is now, and will be
    for ever. Amen. Alleluia.

PSALMODY

Psalm 63:2–9
A soul thirsting for God

*Whoever has left the darkness of sin, yearns for
God.*

O God, you are my God, for you I long;
for you my soul is thirsting.
My body pines for you
like a dry, weary land without water.
So I gaze on you in the sanctuary
to see your strength and your glory.

For your love is better than life,
my lips will speak your praise.
So I will bless you all my life,
in your name I will lift up my hands.
My soul shall be filled as with a banquet,
my mouth shall praise you with joy.

On my bed I remember you.
On you I muse through the night
for you have been my help;
in the shadow of your wings I rejoice.
My soul clings to you;
your right hand holds me fast.

Psalm-prayer

Father, creator of unfailing light, give that
same light to those who call to you. May our lips
praise you; our lives proclaim your goodness; our
work give you honor, and our voices celebrate
you for ever.

Ant. 2 Our Redeemer has risen from the tomb;
let us sing a hymn of praise to the Lord
our God, alleluia.

CANTICLE   *Daniel 3:57–88, 56*
Let all creatures praise the Lord

All you servants of the Lord, sing praise to him
(Revelation 19:5).

Bless the Lord, all you works of the Lord.
Praise and exalt him above all forever.
Angels of the Lord, bless the Lord.
You heavens, bless the Lord.
All you waters above the heavens, bless the
   Lord.
All you hosts of the Lord, bless the Lord.

Sun and moon, bless the Lord.
Stars of heaven, bless the Lord.

Every shower and dew, bless the Lord.
All you winds, bless the Lord.
Fire and heat, bless the Lord.
Cold and chill, bless the Lord.
Dew and rain, bless the Lord.
Frost and chill, bless the Lord.
Ice and snow, bless the Lord.
Nights and days, bless the Lord.

Ant. 3   Alleluia, the Lord is risen as he promised, alleluia.

Psalm 149
The joy of God's holy people

Let the sons of the Church, the children of the new people, rejoice in Christ, their King (Hesychius).

Sing a new song to the Lord,
his praise in the assembly of the faithful.
Let Israel rejoice in its maker,
let Zion's sons exult in their king.
Let them praise his name with dancing
and make music with timbrel and harp.

For the Lord takes delight in his people.
He crowns the poor with salvation.
Let the faithful rejoice in their glory,

shout for joy and take their rest.
Let the praise of God be on their lips
and a two-edged sword in their hand,

to deal out vengeance to the nations
and punishment on all the peoples;
to bind their kings in chains
and their nobles in fetters of iron;
to carry out the sentence pre-ordained;
this honor is for all his faithful.

Psalm-prayer

Let Israel rejoice in you, Lord, and acknowledge you as creator and redeemer. We put our
trust in your faithfulness and proclaim the wonderful truths of salvation. May your loving kindness embrace us now and for ever.

READING   *Acts 10:40–43*

God raised up Jesus on the third day and
granted that he be seen, not by all, but only by
such witnesses as had been chosen beforehand
by God—by us who ate and drank with him after
he rose from the dead. He commissioned us to
preach to the people and to bear witness that he
is the one set apart by God as judge of the living
and the dead. To him all the prophets testify,
saying that everyone who believes in him has
forgiveness of sins through his name.

IN PLACE OF THE RESPONSORY THE FOLLOWING IS SAID:

Ant. **This is the day the Lord has made; let us rejoice and be glad, alleluia.**

CANTICLE OF ZECHARIAH

Ant. **Very early on the morning after the Sabbath, when the sun had just risen, they came to the tomb, alleluia.**

INTERCESSIONS

Christ is the Lord of life, raised up by the Father; in his turn he will raise us up by his power. Let us pray to him, saying:
Christ our life, save us.
Lord Jesus, light shining in the darkness, you lead your people into life, and give our mortal nature the gift of holiness,
—may we spend this day in praise of your glory.
Lord, you walked the way of suffering and crucifixion,
—may we suffer and die with you, and rise again to share your glory.
Son of the Father, our master and our brother, you have made us a kingdom of priests for our God,
—may we offer you our joyful sacrifice of praise.

King of glory, we look forward to the great day
of your coming in splendor,
—that we may see you face to face, and be
transformed in your likeness.

Our Father . . .

PRAYER

God our Father,
by raising Christ your Son
you conquered the power of death
and opened for us the way to eternal life.

Let our celebration today
raise us up and renew our lives
by the Spirit that is within us.

Grant this through our Lord Jesus Christ, your
Son,
who lives and reigns with you and the Holy
Spirit,
one God, for ever and ever.

May the Lord bless us,
protect us from all evil
and bring us to everlasting life.
—Amen.

EVENING PRAYER

God, come to my assistance.
—Lord, make haste to help me.

Glory to the Father, and to the Son, and to the
  Holy Spirit:
as it was in the beginning, is now, and will be
  for ever. Amen. Alleluia.

PSALMODY

Ant. 1   **Mary Magdalene and the other Mary
           came to see the Lord's tomb, alleluia.**

Psalm 110:1–5, 7

The Lord's revelation to my Master:
"Sit on my right:
your foes I will put beneath your feet."

The Lord will wield from Zion
your scepter of power:
rule in the midst of all your foes.

A prince from the day of your birth
on the holy mountains;
from the womb before the dawn I begot you.

The Lord has sworn an oath he will not
  change.
"You are a priest for ever,
a priest like Melchizedek of old."

The Master standing at your right hand
will shatter kings in the day of his great wrath.

He shall drink from the stream by the wayside
and therefore he shall lift up his head.

Ant. 2   **Come and see the place where the Lord
was buried, alleluia.**

Psalm 114

When Israel came forth from Egypt,
Jacob's sons from an alien people,
Judah became the Lord's temple,
Israel became his kingdom.

The sea fled at the sight:
the Jordan turned back on its course,
the mountains leapt like rams
and the hills like yearling sheep.

Why was it, sea, that you fled,
that you turned back, Jordan, on your course?
Mountains, that you leapt like rams,
hills, like yearling sheep?

Tremble, O earth, before the Lord,
in the presence of the God of Jacob,
who turns the rock into a pool
and flint into a spring of water.

Ant. 3　**Jesus said: Do not be afraid. Go and tell my brothers to set out for Galilee; there they will see me, alleluia.**

CANTICLE　　　　　　　　　　　*Revelation 19:1–7*

Alleluia.
Salvation, glory, and power to our God:
(R. **Alleluia.**)
his judgments are honest and true.
R. **Alleluia (alleluia).**

Alleluia.
Sing praise to our God, all you his servants,
(R. **Alleluia.**)
all who worship him reverently, great and small.
R. **Alleluia (alleluia).**

Alleluia.
The Lord our all-powerful God is King;
(R. **Alleluia.**)
let us rejoice, sing praise, and give him glory.
R. **Alleluia (alleluia).**

Alleluia.
The wedding feast of the Lamb has begun,
(R. **Alleluia.**)
and his bride is prepared to welcome him.
R. **Alleluia (alleluia).**

READING   *Hebrews 10:12–14*

Jesus offered one sacrifice for sins and took his seat forever at the right hand of God; now he waits until his enemies are placed beneath his feet. By one offering he has forever perfected those who are being sanctified.

IN PLACE OF THE RESPONSORY THE FOLLOWING IS SAID:

Ant.   **This is the day the Lord has made; let us rejoice and be glad, alleluia.**

CANTICLE OF MARY

Ant.   **On the evening of the first day of the week, the disciples were gathered together behind locked doors; suddenly, Jesus stood among them and said: Peace be with you, alleluia.**

INTERCESSIONS

With joy in our hearts, let us call upon Christ the Lord, who died and rose again, and lives always to intercede for us:
Victorious King, hear our prayer.
Light and salvation of all peoples,
—send into our hearts the fire of your Spirit, as we proclaim your resurrection.
Let Israel recognize in you her longed-for Messiah,

—and the whole earth be filled with the knowledge of your glory.

Keep us in the communion of your saints,

—and grant us rest from our labors in their company.

You have triumphed over death, your enemy; destroy in us the power of death,

—that we may live only for you, victorious and immortal Lord.

Savior Christ, you were obedient even to accepting death, and we were raised up to the right hand of the Father,

—in your goodness welcome your brothers and sisters into the kingdom of your glory.

Our Father . . .

PRAYER

God our Father, creator of all,
today is the day of Easter joy.
This is the morning on which the Lord appeared to men
who had begun to lose hope
and opened their eyes to what the scriptures foretold:
that first he must die, and then he would rise
and ascend into his Father's glorious presence.
May the risen Lord
breathe on our minds and open our eyes

that we may know him in the breaking of
   bread,
and follow him in his risen life.

Grant this through Christ our Lord.

May the Lord bless us,
protect us from all evil
and bring us to everlasting life.
—Amen.

MORNING PRAYER

God, come to my assistance.
—Lord, make haste to help me.

Glory to the Father, and to the Son, and to the
  Holy Spirit:
as it was in the beginning, is now, and will be
  for ever. Amen. Alleluia.

Ant. 1 You have filled me with gladness, Lord;
        I will sing for joy at the works of your
        hands, Alleluia.

Psalm 92
Praise of God the Creator
Sing in praise of Christ's redeeming work (Saint
Athanasius).

It is good to give thanks to the Lord,
to make music to your name, O Most High,
to proclaim your love in the morning
and your truth in the watches of the night,

on the ten-stringed lyre and the lute,
with the murmuring sound of the harp.

Your deeds, O Lord, have made me glad;
for the work of your hands I shout with joy.

109

O Lord, how great are your works!
How deep are your designs!
The foolish man cannot know this
and the fool cannot understand.

Though the wicked spring up like grass
and all who do evil thrive:
they are doomed to be eternally destroyed.
But you, Lord, are eternally on high.
See how your enemies perish;
all doers of evil are scattered.

To me you give the wild-ox's strength;
you anoint me with the purest oil.
My eyes looked in triumph on my foes;
my ears heard gladly of their fall.
The just will flourish like the palm-tree
and grow like a Lebanon cedar.

Planted in the house of the Lord
they will flourish in the courts of our God,
still bearing fruit when they are old,
still full of sap, still green,
to proclaim that the Lord is just;
in him, my rock, there is no wrong.

Psalm-prayer

Take our shame away from us, Lord, and make
us rejoice in your saving works. May all who

have been chosen by your Son always abound in
works of faith, hope and love in your service.

Ant. 2   **It is I who bring death and I who give
         life; I inflict injury and I bring healing,
         alleluia.**

CANTICLE   *Deuteronomy 32:1–12*
    God's kindness to his people

*How often I have longed to gather your children
as a hen gathers her brood under her wing* (Matthew 23:37).

> Give ear, O heavens, while I speak;
>   let the earth hearken to the words of my
>   mouth!
> May my instruction soak in like the rain,
> and my discourse permeate like the dew,
> like a downpour upon the grass,
> like a shower upon the crops:
>
> For I will sing the Lord's renown.
> Oh, proclaim the greatness of our God!
> The Rock—how faultless are his deeds,
> how right all his ways!
> A faithful God, without deceit,
> how just and upright he is!
>
> Yet basely has he been treated by his degener-
>   ate children,

a perverse and crooked race!
Is the Lord to be thus repaid by you,
O stupid and foolish people?
Is he not your father who created you?
Has he not made you and established you?

Think back on the days of old,
reflect on the years of age upon age.
Ask your father and he will inform you,
ask your elders and they will tell you:

When the Most High assigned the nations
    their heritage,
when he parceled out the descendants of
    Adam,
he set up the boundaries of the peoples
after the number of the sons of God;
while the Lord's own portion was Jacob,
his hereditary share was Israel.

He found them in a wilderness,
a wasteland of howling desert.
He shielded them and cared for them,
guarding them as the apple of his eye.

As an eagle incites its nestlings forth
by hovering over its brood,
so he spread his wings to receive them
and bore them up on his pinions.
The Lord alone was their leader,
no strange god was with him.

Ant. 3 **You have crowned your Anointed One
with glory and honor, alleluia.**

Psalm 8
The majesty of the Lord and man's dignity

*The Father gave Christ lordship of creation
and made him head of the Church* (Ephesians
1:22).

How great is your name, O Lord our God,
through all the earth!

Your majesty is praised above the heavens;
on the lips of children and of babes
you have found praise to foil your enemy,
to silence the foe and the rebel.

When I see the heavens, the work of your
    hands,
the moon and the stars which you arranged,
what is man that you should keep him in
    mind,
mortal man that you care for him?

Yet you have made him little less than a god;
with glory and honor you crowned him,
gave him power over the works of your hand,
put all things under his feet.

All of them, sheep and cattle,
yes, even the savage beasts,—

birds of the air, and fish
that make their way through the waters.

How great is your name, O Lord our God,
through all the earth!

Psalm-prayer

Almighty Lord, how wonderful is your name.
You have made every creature subject to you;
make us worthy to give you service.

READING   *Romans 14:7–9*

None of us lives as his own master and none of
us dies as his own master. While we live we are
responsible to the Lord, and when we die we die
as his servants. Both in life and death we are the
Lord's. That is why Christ died and came to life
again, that he might be Lord of both the dead
and the living.

RESPONSORY

The Lord is risen from the tomb, alleluia, al-
    leluia.
—The Lord is risen from the tomb, alleluia,
    alleluia.

He hung upon the cross for us,
—alleluia, alleluia.

Glory to the Father . . .
—The Lord is . . .

CANTICLE OF ZECHARIAH

Ant. **Peace be with you; it is I, alleluia; do not be
afraid, alleluia.**

INTERCESSIONS

**Christ has made known to us the life that lasts
for ever.**
**With faith and joy let us cry out to him, say-
ing:**
*Lord, may your resurrection bring us the
riches of your grace.*
**Eternal shepherd, look on your flock as it rises
from sleep,**
**—feed us with the word of life and the bread
from heaven.**
Keep us safe from wolf and hireling,
**—and make us faithful in listening to your
voice.**
**You are present to all who preach your Gospel,
and give power to their words,**
**—make us today preachers of your resurrec-
tion by our holiness of life.**
**Be our great joy that no one can take from
us,**

—so that we may reject sin with its sadness,
and reach out to eternal life.

Our Father . . .

PRAYER

God our Father,
look upon us with love.
You redeem us and make us your children in
  Christ.
Give us true freedom
and bring us to the inheritance you promised.

We ask this through our Lord Jesus Christ,
  your Son,
who lives and reigns with you and the Holy
  Spirit,
one God, for ever and ever.

May the Lord bless us,
protect us from all evil
and bring us to everlasting life.
—Amen.

EVENING PRAYER

God, come to my assistance.
—Lord, make haste to help me.

Glory to the Father, and to the Son, and to the
   Holy Spirit:
as it was in the beginning, is now, and will be
   for ever. Amen. Alleluia.

PSALMODY

Ant. 1   The Lord our God is high above the heav-
         ens; he raises up the lowly from the dust,
         alleluia.

Psalm 113
Praise the name of the Lord

*He has cast down the mighty and has lifted up
the lowly* (Luke 1:52).

Praise, O servants of the Lord,
praise the name of the Lord!
May the name of the Lord be blessed
both now and for evermore!
From the rising of the sun to its setting
praised be the name of the Lord!

High above all nations is the Lord,
above the heavens his glory.—

Who is like the Lord, our God,
who has risen on high to his throne
yet stoops from the heights to look down,
to look down upon heaven and earth?

From the dust he lifts up the lowly,
from his misery he raises the poor
to set him in the company of princes,
yes, with the princes of his people.
To the childless wife he gives a home
and gladdens her heart with children.

Psalm-prayer

Lord Jesus, Word of God, surrendering the
brightness of your glory you became man so that
we may be raised from the dust to share your
very being. May there be innumerable children
of the Church to offer homage to your name from
the rising of the sun to its setting.

Ant. 2   **Lord, you have broken the chains that
held me bound, I will offer you a sacrifice of praise, alleluia.**

Psalm 116:10–19
Thanksgiving in the Temple

*Through Christ let us offer God a continual sac-
rifice of praise* (Hebrews 13:15).

I trusted, even when I said:
"I am sorely afflicted,"
and when I said in my alarm:
"No man can be trusted."

How can I repay the Lord
for his goodness to me?
The cup of salvation I will raise;
I will call on the Lord's name.

My vows to the Lord I will fulfill
before all his people.
O precious in the eyes of the Lord
is the death of his faithful.

Your servant, Lord, your servant am I;
you have loosened my bonds.
A thanksgiving sacrifice I make:
I will call on the Lord's name.

My vows to the Lord I will fulfill
before all his people,
in the courts of the house of the Lord,
in your midst, O Jerusalem.

Psalm-prayer

Father, precious in your sight is the death of
the saints, but precious above all is the love with
which Christ suffered to redeem us. In this life
we fill up in our own flesh what is still lacking

in the sufferings of Christ; accept this as our sacrifice of praise, and we shall even now taste the
joy of the new Jerusalem.

Ant. 3   Though he was the Son of God, Christ
learned obedience through suffering;
and for all who obey him, he has become
the source of life, alleluia.

CANTICLE   *Philippians 2:6–11*
Christ, God's holy servant

Though he was in the form of God,
Jesus did not deem equality with God
something to be grasped at.

Rather, he emptied himself
and took the form of a slave,
being born in the likeness of men.

He was known to be of human estate,
and it was thus that he humbled himself,
obediently accepting even death,
death on a cross!

Because of this,
God highly exalted him
and bestowed on him the name
above every other name,

So that at Jesus' name
every knee must bend

in the heavens, on the earth,
and under the earth,
and every tongue proclaim
to the glory of God the Father:
JESUS CHRIST IS LORD!

READING

You are "a chosen race, a royal priesthood, a holy nation, a people he claims for his own to proclaim the glorious works" of the One who called you from darkness into his marvelous light. Once you were no people, but now you are God's people; once there was no mercy for you, but now you have found mercy.

RESPONSORY

The disciples rejoiced, alleluia, alleluia.
—The disciples rejoiced, alleluia, alleluia.

When they saw the risen Lord,
—alleluia, alleluia.

Glory to the Father . . .
—The disciples rejoiced . . .

CANTICLE OF MARY

Ant.   Stay with us, Lord, for evening draws near and daylight is fading, alleluia.

INTERCESSIONS

Christ is our life and resurrection. Let us cry out to him with faith:
Son of the living God, protect your people.
Lord Jesus, we pray for your Catholic Church,
—make it holy, so that your kingdom may be established among all nations.
We pray for the sick and the sorrowful, for those in bondage and in exile,
—that they may receive consolation and help.
We pray for those who have turned away from your paths,
—that they may experience the grace of your forgiveness and the joy of rising to new life.
Crucified and risen Savior, you will come to judge the world,
—have mercy on us sinners.
We pray for all the living,
—and for all who have gone from us in the hope of resurrection.

Our Father . . .

PRAYER

God our Father,
may we look forward with hope to our resurrection,

for you have made us your sons and daughters,
and restored the joy of our youth.

We ask this through our Lord Jesus Christ,
  your Son,
who lives and reigns with you and the Holy
  Spirit,
one God, for ever and ever.

May the Lord bless us,
protect us from all evil
and bring us to everlasting life.
—Amen.

Pentecost

. . . send your Spirit
into our lives. . . .

**THIS SECTION MAY BE PRAYED
ON PENTECOST AND WHEN ONE WISHES
TO PRAY TO THE HOLY SPIRIT.**

MORNING PRAYER

God, come to my assistance.
—Lord, make haste to help me.

Glory to the Father, and to the Son, and to the
    Holy Spirit:
as it was in the beginning, is now, and will be
    for ever. Amen. Alleluia.

PSALMODY

Ant. 1   O Lord, how good and gentle is your
         Spirit in us, alleluia.

Psalm 63:2–9
A soul thirsting for God

Whoever has left the darkness of sin, yearns for
God.

O God, you are my God, for you I long;
for you my soul is thirsting.
My body pines for you
like a dry, weary land without water.
So I gaze on you in the sanctuary
to see your strength and your glory.

For your love is better than life,
my lips will speak your praise.
So I will bless you all my life,
in your name I will lift up my hands.

127

My soul shall be filled as with a banquet,
my mouth shall praise you with joy.

On my bed I remember you.
On you I muse through the night
for you have been my help;
in the shadow of your wings I rejoice.
My soul clings to you;
your right hand holds me fast.

Psalm-prayer

Father, creator of unfailing light, give that same light to those who call to you. May our lips praise you; our lives proclaim your goodness; our work give you honor, and our voices celebrate you for ever.

Ant. 2   Let streams and rivers and all creatures
that live in the waters sing praise to God,
alleluia.

CANTICLE   *Daniel 3:57–88, 56*
Let all creatures praise the Lord

All you servants of the Lord, sing praise to him
(Revelation 19:5).

Bless the Lord, all you works of the Lord.
Praise and exalt him above all forever.
Angels of the Lord, bless the Lord.
You heavens, bless the Lord.

All you waters above the heavens, bless the
    Lord.
All you hosts of the Lord, bless the Lord.
Sun and moon, bless the Lord.
Stars of heaven, bless the Lord.

Every shower and dew, bless the Lord.
All you winds, bless the Lord.
Fire and heat, bless the Lord.
Cold and chill, bless the Lord.
Dew and rain, bless the Lord.
Frost and chill, bless the Lord.
Ice and snow, bless the Lord.
Nights and days, bless the Lord.
Light and darkness, bless the Lord.
Lightnings and clouds, bless the Lord.

Let the earth bless the Lord.
Praise and exalt him above all forever.
Mountains and hills, bless the Lord.
Everything growing from the earth, bless the
    Lord.
You springs, bless the Lord.
Seas and rivers, bless the Lord.
You dolphins and all water creatures, bless the
    Lord.
All you birds of the air, bless the Lord.
All you beasts, wild and tame, bless the Lord.
You sons of men, bless the Lord.

O Israel, bless the Lord.
Praise and exalt him above all forever.
Priests of the Lord, bless the Lord.
Servants of the Lord, bless the Lord.
Spirits and souls of the just, bless the Lord.
Holy men of humble heart, bless the Lord.
Hananiah, Azariah, Mishael, bless the Lord.
Praise and exalt him above all forever.

Let us bless the Father, and the Son, and the
Holy Spirit.
Let us praise and exalt him above all forever.
Blessed are you, Lord, in the firmament of
heaven.
Praiseworthy and glorious and exalted above
all forever.

AT THE END OF THE CANTICLE THE GLORY TO THE FATHER IS NOT
SAID.

Ant. 3 **The apostles preached in different
tongues, and proclaimed the great
works of God, alleluia.**

Psalm 149
The joy of God's holy people

*Let the sons of the Church, the children of the
new people, rejoice in Christ, their King* (Hesychius).

Sing a new song to the Lord,
his praise in the assembly of the faithful.
Let Israel rejoice in its maker,
let Zion's sons exult in their king.
Let them praise his name with dancing
and make music with timbrel and harp.

For the Lord takes delight in his people.
He crowns the poor with salvation.
Let the faithful rejoice in their glory,
shout for joy and take their rest.
Let the praise of God be on their lips
and a two-edged sword in their hand,

to deal out vengeance to the nations
and punishment on all the peoples;
to bind their kings in chains
and their nobles in fetters of iron;
to carry out the sentence pre-ordained;
this honor is for all his faithful.

Psalm-prayer

Let Israel rejoice in you, Lord, and acknowledge you as creator and redeemer. We put our trust in your faithfulness and proclaim the wonderful truths of salvation. May your loving kindness embrace us now and for ever.

READING   *Acts 5:30–32*

The God of our fathers has raised up Jesus
whom you put to death, hanging him on a tree.
He whom God has exalted at his right hand as
ruler and savior is to bring repentance to Israel
and forgiveness of sins. We testify to this. So too
does the Holy Spirit, whom God has given to
those that obey him.

RESPONSORY

All were filled with the Holy Spirit, alleluia,
    alleluia.
—All were filled with the Holy Spirit, alleluia,
    alleluia.

They began to speak,
—alleluia, alleluia.

Glory to the Father . . .
—All were filled . . .

CANTICLE OF ZECHARIAH

Ant.   Receive the Holy Spirit; the sins of those
        you forgive shall be forgiven, alleluia.

INTERCESSIONS

Christ the Lord has gathered his Church in
    unity through the Spirit. With sure hope let
    us ask him:

Lord, make the whole world new.

Lord Jesus, when you were raised high upon the cross, streams of living water flowed from your pierced side,

—pour out on us your life-giving Spirit.

In glory at the right hand of God, you gave the Gift of the Father to your disciples,

—send forth your Spirit to renew the world.

You gave your Spirit to the apostles, with the power to forgive sins,

—destroy all sin in the world.

You promised us the Holy Spirit, to teach us all things and remind us of all you had said,

—send us your Spirit to enlighten our minds in faith.

You promised to send the Spirit of truth, to bear witness to yourself,

—send forth your Spirit to make us your faithful witnesses.

Our Father . . .

Prayer

God our Father,
let the Spirit you sent on your Church
to begin the teaching of the gospel
continue to work in the world
through the hearts of all who believe.

We ask this through our Lord Jesus Christ,
   your Son,
who lives and reigns with you and the Holy
   Spirit,
one God, for ever and ever.

May the Lord bless us,
protect us from all evil
and bring us to everlasting life.
—Amen.

EVENING PRAYER

God, come to my assistance.
—Lord, make haste to help me.

Glory to the Father, and to the Son, and to the
  Holy Spirit:
as it was in the beginning, is now, and will be
  for ever. Amen. Alleluia.

Ant. 1   The Spirit of the Lord has filled the
         whole world, alleluia.

Psalm 110:1–5, 7

The Lord's revelation to my Master:
"Sit on my right:
your foes I will put beneath your feet."

The Lord will wield from Zion
your scepter of power:
rule in the midst of all your foes.

A prince from the day of your birth
on the holy mountains;
from the womb before the dawn I begot you.

The Lord has sworn an oath he will not
  change.
"You are a priest for ever,
a priest like Melchizedek of old."

The Master standing at your right hand
will shatter kings in the day of his wrath.

He shall drink from the stream by the wayside
and therefore he shall lift up his head.

Ant. 2   Send us your strength, O God, from your
          holy temple in Jerusalem, and perfect
          your work in us, alleluia.

Psalm 114

When Israel came forth from Egypt,
Jacob's sons from an alien people,
Judah became the Lord's temple,
Israel became his kingdom.

The sea fled at the sight:
the Jordan turned back on its course,
the mountains leapt like rams
and the hills like yearling sheep.

Why was it, sea, that you fled,
that you turned back, Jordan, on your course?
Mountains, that you leapt like rams,
hills, like yearling sheep?

Tremble, O earth, before the Lord,
in the presence of the God of Jacob,
who turns the rock into a pool
and flint into a spring of water.

Ant. 3   All were filled with the Holy Spirit, and
         they began to speak, alleluia.

CANTICLE   *Revelation 19:1–7*

Alleluia.
Salvation, glory, and power to our God:
(R.Alleluia.)
his judgments are honest and true.
R.Alleluia (alleluia).

Alleluia.
Sing praise to our God, all you his servants,
(R.Alleluia.)
all who worship him reverently, great and
    small.
R.Alleluia (alleluia).

Alleluia.
The Lord our all-powerful God is King;
(R.Alleluia.)
let us rejoice, sing praise, and give him glory.
R.Alleluia (alleluia).

Alleluia.
The wedding feast of the Lamb has begun,
(R.Alleluia.)
and his bride is prepared to welcome him.
R.Alleluia (alleluia).

READING   *Ephesians 4:3–6*

Make every effort to preserve the unity which
has the Spirit as its origin and peace as its bind-
ing force. There is but one body and one Spirit,
just as there is but one hope given all of you by
your call. There is one Lord, one faith, one baptism; one God and Father of all, who is over all,
and works through all, and is in all.

RESPONSORY

The Spirit of the Lord has filled the whole
   world, alleluia, alleluia.
—The Spirit of the Lord has filled the whole
   world, alleluia, alleluia.

He sustains all creation and knows every word
   that is spoken,
—alleluia, alleluia.

Glory to the Father . . .
—The Spirit of . . .

CANTICLE OF MARY

Ant.   Today we celebrate the feast of Pentecost,
       alleluia; on this day the Holy Spirit ap-
       peared before the apostles in tongues of
       fire and gave them his spiritual gifts. He
       sent them out to preach to the whole

world, and to proclaim that all who believe and are baptized shall be saved, alleluia.

INTERCESSIONS

God the Father has gathered his Church in
   unity through Christ. With joy in our hearts
   let us ask him:
   Send your Holy Spirit into the Church.
You desire the unity of all Christians through
   one baptism in the Spirit,
make all who believe one in heart and soul.
You desire the whole world to be filled with the
   Spirit,
help all mankind to build a world of justice
   and peace.
Lord God, Father of all mankind, you desire to
   gather together your scattered children in
   unity of faith,
—enlighten the world by the grace of the Holy
   Spirit.
Through the Spirit you make all things new,
—heal the sick, comfort the distressed, give
   salvation to all.
Through the Spirit you raised your Son from
   the dead,
—raise up the bodies of the dead into everlasting life.

Our Father . . .

PRAYER

God our Father,
let the Spirit you sent on your Church
to begin the teaching of the gospel
continue to work in the world
through the hearts of all who believe.

We ask this through our Lord Jesus Christ,
   your Son,
who lives and reigns with you and the Holy
   Spirit,
one God, for ever and ever.

May the Lord bless us,
protect us from all evil
and bring us to everlasting life.
—Amen.

Ordinary Time

. . . come let us worship the Lord . . .

**THIS SECTION MAY BE PRAYED
THROUGHOUT THE YEAR
OUTSIDE OF THE MAJOR LITURGICAL SEASONS.**

Sunday Morning Prayer

God, come to my assistance.
—Lord, make haste to help me.

Glory to the Father, and to the Son, and to the
  Holy Spirit:
as it was in the beginning, is now, and will be
  for ever.
  Amen. Alleluia.

PSALMODY

Ant. 1   As morning breaks I look to you, O God,
             to be my strength this day, alleluia.

Psalm 63:2–9
A soul thirsting for God

*Whoever has left the darkness of sin, yearns for
God.*

O God, you are my God, for you I long;
for you my soul is thirsting.
My body pines for you
like a dry, weary land without water.
So I gaze on you in the sanctuary
to see your strength and your glory.

For your love is better than life,
my lips will speak your praise.
So I will bless you all my life,

143

in your name I will lift up my hands.
My soul shall be filled as with a banquet,
my mouth shall praise you with joy.

On my bed I remember you.
On you I muse through the night
for you have been my help;
in the shadow of your wings I rejoice.
My soul clings to you;
your right hand holds me fast.

Psalm-prayer

Father, creator of unfailing light, give that same light to those who call to you. May our lips praise you; our lives proclaim your goodness; our works give you honor, and our voices celebrate you for ever.

Ant. 2   From the midst of the flames the three young men cried out with one voice: Blessed be God, alleluia.

CANTICLE   *Daniel 3:57–88, 56*
Let all creatures praise the Lord

All you servants of the Lord, sing praise to him
(Revelation 19:5).

Bless the Lord, all you works of the Lord.
Praise and exalt him above all forever.

Angels of the Lord, bless the Lord.
All you waters above the heavens, bless the
    Lord.
All you hosts of the Lord, bless the Lord.
Sun and moon, bless the Lord.
Stars of heaven, bless the Lord.

Every shower and dew, bless the Lord.
All you winds, bless the Lord.
Fire and heat, bless the Lord.
Cold and chill, bless the Lord.
Dew and rain, bless the Lord.
Frost and chill, bless the Lord.
Ice and snow, bless the Lord.
Nights and days, bless the Lord.
Light and darkness, bless the Lord.
Lightnings and clouds, bless the Lord.

Let the earth bless the Lord.
Praise and exalt him above all forever.
Mountains and hills, bless the Lord.
Everything growing from the earth, bless the
    Lord.
You springs, bless the Lord.
Seas and rivers, bless the Lord.
You dolphins and all water creatures, bless the
    Lord.
All you birds of the air, bless the Lord.

All you beasts, wild and tame, bless the Lord.
You sons of men, bless the Lord.

O Israel, bless the Lord.
Praise and exalt him above all forever.
Priests of the Lord, bless the Lord.
Servants of the Lord, bless the Lord.
Spirits and souls of the just, bless the Lord.
Holy men of humble heart, bless the Lord.
Hananiah, Azariah, Mishael, bless the Lord.
Praise and exalt him above all forever.

Let us bless the Father, and the Son, and the
    Holy Spirit.
Let us praise and exalt him above all forever.
Blessed are you, Lord, in the firmament of
    heaven.
Praiseworthy and glorious and exalted above
    all forever.

Ant. 3   Let the people of Zion rejoice in their
          King, alleluia.

Psalm 149
The joy of God's holy people

*Let the sons of the Church, the children of the
new people, rejoice in Christ, their King* (Hesychius).

Sing a new song to the Lord,
his praise in the assembly of the faithful.

Let Israel rejoice in its maker,
let Zion's sons exult in their king.
Let them praise his name with dancing
and make music with timbrel and harp.

For the Lord takes delight in his people.
He crowns the poor with salvation.
Let the faithful rejoice in their glory,
shout for joy and take their rest.
Let the praise of God be on their lips
and a two-edged sword in their hand,

to deal out vengeance to the nations
and punishment on all the peoples;
to bind their kings in chains
and their nobles in fetters of iron;
to carry out the sentence pre-ordained;
this honor is for all his faithful.

Psalm-prayer

Let Israel rejoice in you, Lord, and acknowledge you as creator and redeemer. We put our trust in your faithfulness and proclaim the wonderful truths of salvation. May your loving kindness embrace us now and for ever.

READING   *Revelation 7:9–12*

I saw before me a huge crowd which no one could count from every nation and race, people and tongue. They stood before the throne and the Lamb, dressed in long white robes and holding palm branches in their hands. They cried out in a loud voice, "Salvation is from our God, who is seated on the throne, and from the Lamb!" All the angels who were standing around the throne and the elders and the four living creatures fell down before the throne to worship God. They said: "Amen! Praise and glory, wisdom and thanksgiving and honor, power and might, to our God forever and ever. Amen!"

RESPONSORY

Christ, Son of the living God, have mercy on us.
—Christ, Son of the living God, have mercy on us.

You are seated at the right hand of the Father,
—have mercy on us.

Glory to the Father . . .
—Christ, Son of . . .

CANTICLE OF ZECHARIAH

Ant.　No one pours new wine into old wineskins; new wine should be put in new wineskins.

INTERCESSIONS

Christ is the sun that never sets, the true light
that shines on every man. Let us call out to
him in praise:
Lord, you are our life and our salvation.
Creator of the stars, we thank you for your gift,
the first rays of the dawn,
—and we commemorate your resurrection.
May your Holy Spirit teach us to do your will
today,
—and may your Wisdom guide us always.

Each Sunday give us the joy of gathering as
your people,
—around the table of your word and your body.
From our hearts we thank you,
—for your countless blessings.

Our Father . . .

PRAYER

Lord,
guide the course of the world events
and give your Church the joy and peace
of serving you in freedom.

We ask this through our Lord Jesus Christ,
your Son,

who lives and reigns with you and the Holy
  Spirit,
one God, for ever and ever.

May the Lord bless us,
protect us from all evil
and bring us to everlasting life.
—Amen.

SUNDAY EVENING PRAYER

God, come to my assistance.
—Lord, make haste to help me.

Glory to the Father, and to the Son, and to the
    Holy Spirit:
as it was in the beginning, is now, and will be
    for ever.
    Amen. Alleluia.

Ant. 1   The Lord will stretch forth his mighty
          scepter from Zion, and he will reign for
          ever, alleluia.

Psalm 110:1–5, 7
The Messiah, king and priest

*Christ's reign will last until all his enemies are
made subject to him* (1 Corinthians 15:25).

The Lord's revelation to my Master:
"Sit on my right:
your foes I will put beneath your feet."

The Lord will wield from Zion
your scepter of power:
rule in the midst of all your foes.

A prince from the day of your birth
on the holy mountains;

from the womb before the dawn I begot
you.

The Lord has sworn an oath he will not
change.
"You are a priest for ever,
a priest like Melchizedek of old."

The Master standing at your right hand
will shatter kings in the day of his great wrath.

He shall drink from the stream by the wayside
and therefore he shall lift up his head.

Psalm-prayer

Father, we ask you to give us victory and
peace. In Jesus Christ, our Lord and King, we are
already seated at your right hand. We look forward to praising you in the fellowship of all your
saints in our heavenly homeland.

Ant. 2   The earth is shaken to its depths before
the glory of your face.

Psalm 114
The Israelites are delivered from the bondage
of Egypt
*You too left Egypt when, at baptism, you re-
nounced that world which is at enmity with
God* (Saint Augustine).

When Israel came forth from Egypt,
Jacob's sons from an alien people,
Judah became the Lord's temple,
Israel became his kingdom.

The sea fled at the sight:
the Jordan turned back on its course,
the mountains leapt like rams
and the hills like yearling sheep.

Why was it, sea, that you fled,
that you turned back, Jordan, on your course?
Mountains, that you leapt like rams,
hills, like yearling sheep?

Tremble, O earth, before the Lord,
in the presence of the God of Jacob,
who turns the rock into a pool
and flint into a spring of water.

Psalm-prayer

Almighty God, ever-living mystery of unity
and trinity, you gave life to the new Israel by
birth from water and the Spirit, and made it a
chosen race, a royal priesthood, a people set
apart as your eternal possession. May all those
you have called to walk in the splendor of the
new light render you fitting service and adoration.

Ant. 3 **All power is yours, Lord God, our mighty King, alleluia.**

CANTICLE *Revelation 19:1–7*

The wedding of the Lamb

Alleluia.
Salvation, glory, and power to our God:
(Alleluia.)
his judgments are honest and true.
Alleluia (Alleluia).

Alleluia.
Sing praise to our God, all you his servants,
(Alleluia.)
all who worship him reverently, great and small.
Alleluia (alleluia).

Alleluia.
The Lord our all-powerful God is King;
Alleluia.
let us rejoice, sing praise, and give him glory.
Alleluia (alleluia).

Alleluia.
The wedding feast of the Lamb has begun,
(Alleluia.)
and his bride is prepared to welcome him.
Alleluia, alleluia. Alleluia, alleluia.

READING   *2 Corinthians 1:3–7*

Praised be God, the Father of our Lord Jesus
Christ, the Father of mercies and the God of all
consolation! He comforts us in all our afflictions
and thus enables us to comfort those who are in
trouble, with the same consolation we have received from him. As we have shared much in the
suffering of Christ, so through Christ do we
share abundantly in his consolation. If we are
afflicted it is for your encouragement and salvation, and when we are consoled it is for your
consolation, so that you may endure patiently
the same sufferings we endure. Our hope for you
is firm because we know that just as you share in
the sufferings, so you will share in the consolation.

RESPONSORY

The whole creation proclaims the greatness of
   your glory.
—The whole creation proclaims the greatness
   of your glory.
Eternal ages praise
—the greatness of your glory.
Glory to the Father . . .
—The whole creation . . .

CANTICLE OF MARY

Ant. Brothers, if you desire to be truly rich, set your hearts on true riches.

INTERCESSIONS

Christ the Lord is our head; we are his members. In joy let us call out to him:
Lord, may your kingdom come.
Christ our Savior, make your Church a more vivid symbol of the unity of all mankind,
—make it more effectively the sacrament of salvation for all peoples.
Through your presence, guide the college of bishops in union with the Pope,
—give them the gifts of unity, love and peace.
Bind all Christians more closely to yourself, their divine Head,
—lead them to proclaim your kingdom by the witness of their lives.
Grant peace to the world,
—let every land flourish in justice and security.
Grant to the dead the glory of resurrection,
—and give us a share in their happiness.

Our Father . . .

PRAYER

Father of everlasting goodness,
our origin and guide,
be close to us
and hear the prayers of all who praise you.
Forgive our sins and restore us to life.
Keep us safe in your love.

Grant this through our Lord Jesus Christ, your
  Son,
who lives and reigns with you and the Holy
  Spirit, one God, for ever and ever.

May the Lord bless us,
protect us from all evil
and bring us to everlasting life.
—Amen.

MONDAY MORNING PRAYER

God, come to my assistance.
—Lord, make haste to help me.

Glory to the Father, and to the Son, and to the
　　Holy Spirit:
as it was in the beginning, is now, and will be
　　for ever. Amen. Alleluia.

PSALMODY

Ant. 1　　I lift up my heart to you, O Lord, and you
　　　　　will hear my morning prayer.

Psalm 5:2–10, 12–13
A morning prayer asking for help

Those who welcome the Word as the guest of
their hearts will have abiding joy.

To my words give ear, O Lord,
give heed to my groaning.
Attend to the sound of my cries,
my King and my God.

It is you whom I invoke, O Lord.
In the morning you hear me;
in the morning I offer you my prayer,
watching and waiting.

You are no God who loves evil;
no sinner is your guest.

158

The boastful shall not stand their ground
before your face.

You hate all who do evil:
you destroy all who lie.
The deceitful and bloodthirsty man
the Lord detests.

But I through the greatness of your love
have access to your house.
I bow down before your holy temple,
filled with awe.

Lead me, Lord, in your justice,
because of those who lie in wait;
make clear your way before me.

No truth can be found in their mouths,
their heart is all mischief,
their throat a wide-open grave,
all honey their speech.

All those you protect shall be glad
and ring out their joy.
You shelter them; in you they rejoice,
those who love your name.

It is you who bless the just man, Lord:
you surround him with favor as with a
     shield.

Psalm-prayer

Lord, all justice and all goodness come from you; you hate evil and abhor lies. Lead us, your servants, in the path of your justice, so that all who hope in you may rejoice with the Church and in Christ.

Ant. 2 We praise your glorious name, O Lord, our God.

CANTICLE   *1 Chronicles 29:10–13*
Glory and honor are due to God alone

Blessed be the God and Father of our Lord Jesus Christ (Ephesians 1:3).

Blessed may you be, O Lord,
God of Israel our father,
from eternity to eternity.

Yours, O Lord, are grandeur and power,
majesty, splendor, and glory.

For all in heaven and on earth is yours;
yours, O Lord, is the sovereignty:
you are exalted as head over all.

Riches and honor are from you,
and you have dominion over all.
In your hands are power and might;
it is yours to give grandeur and strength to all.

Therefore, our God, we give you thanks
and praise the majesty of your name.

Ant. 3 **Adore the Lord in his holy court.**

Psalm 29
A tribute of praise to the Word of God

*The Father's voice proclaimed: "This is my be-
loved Son"* (Matthew 3:17).

O give the Lord, you sons of God,
give the Lord glory and power;
give the Lord the glory of his name.
Adore the Lord in his holy court.

The Lord's voice resounding on the waters,
the Lord on the immensity of waters;
the voice of the Lord, full of power,
the voice of the Lord, full of splendor.

The Lord's voice shattering the cedars,
the Lord shatters the cedars of Lebanon;
he makes Lebanon leap like a calf
and Sirion like a young wild-ox.

The Lord's voice flashes flames of fire.

The Lord's voice shaking the wilderness,
the Lord shakes the wilderness of Kadesh;
the Lord's voice rending the oak tree
and stripping the forest bare.

The God of glory thunders.
In his temple they all cry: "Glory!"
The Lord sat enthroned over the flood;
the Lord sits as king for ever.

The Lord will give strength to his people,
the Lord will bless his people with peace.

Psalm-prayer

You live for ever, Lord and King. All things of
the earth justly sing your glory and honor.
Strengthen your people against evil, that we may
rejoice in your peace and trust in your eternal
promise.

READING   *2 Thessalonians 3:10b–13*

Anyone who would not work should not eat.
We hear that some of you are unruly, not keeping busy but acting like busy-bodies. We enjoin
all such, and we urge them strongly in the Lord
Jesus Christ, to earn the food they eat by working
quietly. You must never grow weary of doing
what is right, brothers.

RESPONSORY

Blessed be the Lord our God,
blessed from age to age.
—Blessed be the Lord our God,

blessed from age to age.
His marvelous works are beyond compare,
—blessed from age to age.

Glory to the Father . . .
—Blessed be the . . .

CANTICLE OF ZECHARIAH

Ant. **Blessed be the Lord our God.**

INTERCESSIONS

We esteem Christ above all men, for he was
    filled with grace and the Holy Spirit. In faith
    let us implore him:
    Give us your Spirit, Lord.
Grant us a peaceful day,
—when evening comes we will praise you with
    joy and purity of heart.
Let your splendor rest upon us today,
—direct the work of our hands.
May your face shine upon us and keep us in
    peace,
—may your strong arm protect us.
Look kindly on all who put their trust in our
    prayers,
—fill them with every bodily and spiritual
    grace.

Our Father . . .

PRAYER

Father,
may everything we do
begin with your inspiration
and continue with your saving help.
Let our work always find its origin in you
and through you reach completion.

We ask this through our Lord Jesus Christ,
   your Son,
who lives and reigns with you and the Holy
   Spirit,
one God, for ever and ever.

May the Lord bless us,
protect us from all evil
and bring us to everlasting life.
—Amen.

MONDAY EVENING PRAYER

God, come to my assistance.
—Lord, make haste to help me.

Glory to the Father, and to the Son, and to the
   Holy Spirit:
as it was in the beginning, is now, and will be
   for ever. Amen. Alleluia.

PSALMODY

Ant. 1   The Lord looks tenderly on those who are
         poor.

Psalm 11
God is the unfailing support of the just

*Blessed are those who hunger and thirst for jus-
tice; they shall be satisfied* (Matthew 5:6).

In the Lord I have taken my refuge.
How can you say to my soul:
"Fly like a bird to its mountain.

See the wicked bracing their bow;
they are fixing their arrows on the string
to shoot upright men in the dark.
Foundations once destroyed, what can the just
   do?"

The Lord is in his holy temple,
the Lord, whose throne is in heaven.

His eyes look down on the world;
his gaze tests mortal men.

The Lord tests the just and the wicked:
the lover of violence he hates.
He sends fire and brimstone on the wicked;
he sends a scorching wind as their lot.

The Lord is just and loves justice:
the upright shall see his face.

Psalm-prayer

Lord God, you search the hearts of all, both the good and the wicked. May those who are in danger for love of you, find security in you now, and, in the day of judgment, may they rejoice in seeing you face to face.

Ant. 2 **Blessed are the pure of heart, for they shall see God.**

Psalm 15
Who is worthy to stand in God's presence?

You have come to Mount Zion, to the city of the living God (Hebrews 12:22).

Lord, who shall be admitted to your tent
and dwell on your holy mountain?

He who walks without fault;
he who acts with justice

and speaks the truth from his heart;
he who does not slander with his tongue;

he who does no wrong to his brother,
who casts no slur on his neighbor,
who holds the godless in disdain,
but honors those who fear the Lord;

he who keeps his pledge, come what may;
who takes no interest on a loan
and accepts no bribes against the innocent.
Such a man will stand firm for ever.

Psalm-prayer

Make our lives blameless, Lord. Help us to do
what is right and to speak what is true, that we
may dwell in your tent and find rest on your holy
mountain.

Ant. 3 **God chose us in his Son to be his adopted children.**

CANTICLE   *Ephesians 1:3–10*
God our Savior

Praised be the God and Father
of our Lord Jesus Christ,
who has bestowed on us in Christ
every spiritual blessing in the heavens.

God chose us in him
before the world began

to be holy
and blameless in his sight.

He predestined us
to be his adopted sons through Jesus Christ,
such was his will and pleasure,
that all might praise the glorious favor
he has bestowed on us in his beloved.

In him and through his blood, we have been
    redeemed,
and our sins forgiven,
so immeasurably generous
is God's favor to us.

God has given us the wisdom
to understand fully the mystery,
the plan he was pleased
to decree in Christ.

A plan to be carried out
in Christ, in the fullness of time,
to bring all things into one in him,
in the heavens and on earth.

READING   *Colossians 1:9b–13*

May you attain full knowledge of God's will
through perfect wisdom and spiritual insight.
Then you will lead a life worthy of the Lord and
pleasing to him in every way. You will multiply

good works of every sort and grow in the knowledge of God. By the might of his glory you will be endowed with the strength needed to stand fast, even to endure joyfully whatever may come, giving thanks to the Father for having made you worthy to share the lot of the saints in light. He rescued us from the power of darkness and brought us into the kingdom of his beloved Son.

RESPONSORY

Lord, you alone can heal me, for I have grieved you by my sins.
—Lord, you alone can heal me, for I have grieved you by my sins.
Once more I say: O Lord, have mercy on me,
—for I have grieved you by my sins.
Glory to the Father . . .
—Lord, you alone . . .

CANTICLE OF MARY

Ant.   My soul proclaims the greatness of the Lord, for he has looked with favor on his lowly servant.

INTERCESSIONS

God has made an everlasting covenant with his people, and he never ceases to bless

them. Grateful for these gifts, we confidently
direct our prayer to him:
Lord, bless your people.
Save your people, Lord,
—and bless your inheritance.
Gather into one body all who bear the name of
    Christian,
—that the world may believe in Christ whom
    you have sent.
Give our friends and our loved ones a share in
    divine life,
—let them be symbols of Christ before men.
Show your love to those who are suffering,
—open their eyes to the vision of your revela-
    tion.
Be compassionate to those who have died,
—welcome them into the company of the
    faithful departed.

Our Father . . .

PRAYER

Father,
may this evening pledge of our service to you
bring you glory and praise.
For our salvation you looked with favor
on the lowliness of the Virgin Mary;
lead us to the fullness of the salvation
you have prepared for us.

We ask this through our Lord Jesus Christ,
    your Son,
who lives and reigns with you and the Holy
    Spirit,
one God, for ever and ever.

May the Lord bless us,
protect us from all evil
and bring us to everlasting life.
—Amen.

TUESDAY MORNING PRAYER

God, come to my assistance.
—Lord, make haste to help me.

Glory to the Father, and to the Son, and to the
Holy Spirit:
as it was in the beginning, is now, and will be
for ever. Amen. Alleluia.

Ant. 1   The man whose deeds are blameless and
whose heart is pure will climb the
mountain of the Lord.

Psalm 24
The Lord's entry into his temple

*Christ opened heaven for us in the manhood he
assumed* (Saint Irenaeus).

The Lord's is the earth and its fullness,
the world and all its peoples.
It is he who set it on the seas;
on the waters he made it firm.

Who shall climb the mountain of the Lord?
Who shall stand in his holy place?

The man with clean hands and pure heart,
who desires not worthless things,

172

who has not sworn so as to deceive his neighbor.

He shall receive blessings from the Lord
and reward from the God who saves him.
Such are the men who seek him,
seek the face of the God of Jacob.

O gates, lift high your heads;
grow higher, ancient doors.
Let him enter, the king of glory!

Who is the king of glory?
The Lord, the mighty, the valiant,
the Lord, the valiant in war.

O gates, lift high your heads;
grow higher, ancient doors.
Let him enter, the king of glory!

Who is he, the king of glory?
He, the Lord of armies,
he is the king of glory.

Psalm-prayer

King of glory, Lord of power and might,
cleanse our hearts from all sin, preserve the in-
nocence of our hands, and keep our minds from
vanity, so that we may deserve your blessing in
your holy place.

Ant. 2 **Praise the eternal King in all your deeds.**

CANTICLE   *Tobit 13:1–8*
God afflicts but only to heal

Blessed be the God and Father of our Lord Jesus Christ, who in his great love for us has brought us to a new birth (1 Peter 1:3).

Blessed be God who lives forever,
because his kingdom lasts for all ages.

For he scourges and then has mercy;
he casts down to the depths of the nether
    world,
and he brings up from the great abyss.
No one can escape his hand.

Praise him, you Israelites, before the Gentiles,
for though he has scattered you among them,
he has shown you his greatness even there.

Exalt him before every living being,
because he is the Lord our God,
our Father and God forever.

He scourged you for your iniquities,
but will again have mercy on you all.
He will gather you from all the Gentiles
among whom you have been scattered.

When you turn back to him with all your
    heart,

to do what is right before him,
then he will turn back to you,
and no longer hide his face from you.

So now consider what he has done for you,
and praise him with full voice.
Bless the Lord of righteousness,
and exalt the King of the ages.

In the land of my exile I praise him,
and show his power and majesty to a sinful
    nation.
"Turn back, you sinners! do the right before
    him:
perhaps he may look with favor upon you
and show you mercy.

"As for me, I exalt my God,
and my spirit rejoices in the King of heaven.
Let all men speak of his majesty,
and sing his praises in Jerusalem."

Ant. 3 **The loyal heart must praise the Lord.**

Psalm 33
Song of praise for God's continual care

Through the Word all things were made (John
1:3).

Ring out your joy to the Lord, O you just;
for praise is fitting for loyal hearts.

Give thanks to the Lord upon the harp,
with a ten-stringed lute sing him songs.
O sing him a song that is new,
play loudly, with all your skill.

For the word of the Lord is faithful
and all his works to be trusted.
The Lord loves justice and right
and fills the earth with his love.

By his word the heavens were made,
by the breath of his mouth all the stars.
He collects the waves of the ocean;
he stores up the depths of the sea.

Let all the earth fear the Lord,
all who live in the world revere him.
He spoke; and it came to be.
He commanded; it sprang into being.

He frustrates the designs of the nations,
he defeats the plans of the peoples.
His own designs shall stand for ever,
the plans of his heart from age to age.

They are happy, whose God is the Lord,
the people he has chosen as his own.
From the heavens the Lord looks forth,
he sees all the children of men.

From the place where he dwells he gazes
on all the dwellers on the earth,

he who shapes the hearts of them all
and considers all their deeds.

A king is not saved by his army,
nor a warrior preserved by his strength.
A vain hope for safety is the horse;
despite its power it cannot save.

The Lord looks on those who revere him,
on those who hope in his love,
to rescue their souls from death,
to keep them alive in famine.

Our soul is waiting for the Lord.
The Lord is our help and our shield.
In him do our hearts find joy.
We trust in his holy name.

May your love be upon us, O Lord,
as we place all our hope in you.

Psalm-prayer

Nourish your people, Lord, for we hunger for
your word. Rescue us from the death of sin and
fill us with your mercy, that we may share your
presence and the joys of all the saints.

READING   *Romans 13:11–14*

You know the time in which we are living. It
is now the hour for you to wake from sleep, for
our salvation is closer than when we first ac-

cepted the faith. The night is far spent; the day
draws near. Let us cast off deeds of darkness and
put on the armor of light. Let us live honorably
as in daylight; not in carousing and drunken-
ness, not in sexual excess and lust, not in quar-
reling and jealousy. Rather, put on the Lord
Jesus Christ and make no provision for the
desires of the flesh.

RESPONSORY

My God stands by me, all my trust is in
  him.
—My God stands by me, all my trust is in
  him.
I find my refuge in him, and I am truly free;
—all my trust is in him.
Glory to the Father . . .
—My God stands . . .

CANTICLE OF ZECHARIAH

Ant. **God has raised up for us a mighty Savior,
as he promised through the words of his
holy prophets.**

INTERCESSIONS

Beloved brothers and sisters, we share a heavenly calling under Christ, our high priest.

Let us praise him with shouts of joy:
Lord, our God and our Savior.
Almighty King, through baptism you conferred on us a royal priesthood,
—inspire us to offer you a continual sacrifice of praise.
Help us to keep your commandments,
—that through the power of the Holy Spirit we may live in you and you in us.
Give us your eternal wisdom,
—to be with us today and to guide us.
May our companions today be free of sorrow,
—and filled with joy.

Our Father . . .

PRAYER

God our Father,
hear our morning prayer
and let the radiance of your love
scatter the gloom of our hearts.
The light of heaven's love has restored us to life:
free us from the desires that belong to darkness.

We ask this through our Lord Jesus Christ,
your Son,

who lives and reigns with you and the Holy
  Spirit,
one God, for ever and ever.

May the Lord bless us,
protect us from all evil
and bring us to everlasting life.
—Amen.

TUESDAY EVENING PRAYER

God, come to my assistance.
—Lord, make haste to help me.

Glory to the Father, and to the Son, and to the
  Holy Spirit:
as it was in the beginning, is now, and will be
  for ever. Amen. Alleluia.

PSALMODY

Ant. 1   God has crowned his Christ with vic-
         tory.

Psalm 20
A prayer for the king's victory

*Whoever calls upon the name of the Lord will be
saved* (Acts 2:21).

May the Lord answer in time of trial;
may the name of Jacob's God protect you.

May he send you help from his shrine
and give you support from Zion.
May he remember all your offerings
and receive your sacrifice with favor.

May he give you your heart's desire
and fulfill every one of your plans.
May we ring out our joy at your victory

and rejoice in the name of our God.
May the Lord grant all your prayers.

I am sure now that the Lord
will give victory to his anointed,
will reply from his holy heaven
with the mighty victory of his hand.

Some trust in chariots or horses,
but we in the name of the Lord.
They will collapse and fall,
but we shall hold and stand firm.

Give victory to the king, O Lord,
give answer on the day we call.

Psalm-prayer

Lord, you accepted the perfect sacrifice of your
Son upon the cross. Hear us during times of trouble and protect us by the power of his name, that
we who share his struggle on earth may merit a
share in his victory.

Ant. 2 We celebrate your mighty works with
songs of praise, O Lord.

Psalm 21:2–8, 14
Thanksgiving for the king's victory

*He accepted life that he might rise and live for
ever* (Saint Hilary).

O Lord, your strength gives joy to the king;
how your saving help makes him glad!
You have granted him his heart's desire;
you have not refused the prayer of his lips.

You came to meet him with the blessings of
    success,
you have set on his head a crown of pure gold.
He asked you for life and this you have given,
days that will last from age to age.

Your saving help has given him glory.
You have laid upon him majesty and splendor,
you have granted your blessings to him for
    ever.
You have made him rejoice with the joy of
    your presence.

The king has put his trust in the Lord:
through the mercy of the Most High he shall
    stand firm.
O Lord, arise in your strength;
we shall sing and praise your power.

Psalm-prayer

Father, you have given us life on this earth and
have met us with the grace of redemption. Bestow your greatest blessing on us, the fullness of
eternal life.

Ant. 3 **Lord, you have made us a kingdom and priests for God our Father.**

CANTICLE   *Revelation 4:11; 5:9, 10, 12*
                 Redemption hymn

O Lord our God, you are worthy
to receive glory and honor and power.

For you have created all things;
by your will they came to be and were made.

Worthy are you, O Lord,
to receive the scroll and break open its seals.

For you were slain;
with your blood you purchased for God
men of every race and tongue,
of every people and nation.

You made of them a kingdom,
and priests to serve our God,
and they shall reign on the earth.

Worthy is the Lamb that was slain
to receive power and riches,
wisdom and strength,
honor and glory and praise.

READING   *1 John 3:1–3*

See what love the Father has bestowed on us
in letting us be called children of God!

Yet that is what we are.
The reason the world does not recognize us
is that it never recognized the Son.
Dearly beloved,
we are God's children now;
what we shall later be has not yet come to
   light.
We know that when it comes to light
we shall be like him,
for we shall see him as he is.
Everyone who has this hope based on him
keeps himself pure, as he is pure.

RESPONSORY

Through all eternity, O Lord, your promise
   stands unshaken.
—Through all eternity, O Lord, your promise
   stands unshaken.
Your faithfulness will never fail;
—your promise stands unshaken.
Glory to the Father . . .
—Through all eternity . . .

CANTICLE OF MARY

Ant. My spirit rejoices in God my Savior.

INTERCESSIONS

Let us praise Christ the Lord, who lives among
   us, the people he redeemed, and let us say:

Lord, hear our prayer.

Lord, king and ruler of nations, be with all
  your people and their governments,
—inspire them to pursue the good of all according to your law.
You made captive our captivity,
—to our brothers who are enduring bodily or
  spiritual chains, grant the freedom of the
  sons of God.

May our young people be concerned with re-
  maining blameless in your sight,
—and may they generously follow your call.
May our children imitate your example,
—and grow in wisdom and grace.
Accept our dead brothers and sisters into your
  eternal kingdom,
—where we hope to reign with you.

Our Father . . .

PRAYER

Almighty God,
we give you thanks
for bringing us safely
to this evening hour.
May this lifting up of our hands in prayer
be a sacrifice pleasing in your sight.

We ask this through our Lord Jesus Christ,
   your Son,
who lives and reigns with you and the Holy
   Spirit,
one God, for ever and ever.

May the Lord bless us,
protect us from all evil
and bring us to everlasting life.
—Amen.

WEDNESDAY MORNING PRAYER

God, come to my assistance.
—Lord, make haste to help me.

Glory to the Father, and to the Son, and to the
    Holy Spirit:
as it was in the beginning, is now, and will be
    for ever. Amen. Alleluia.

PSALMODY

Ant. 1   O Lord, in your light we see light itself.

Psalm 36
The malice of sinners and God's goodness

*No follower of mine wanders in the dark; he
shall have the light of life* (John 8:12).

Sin speaks to the sinner
in the depths of his heart.
There is no fear of God
before his eyes.

He so flatters himself in his mind
that he knows not his guilt.
In his mouth are mischief and deceit.
All wisdom is gone.

He plots the defeat of goodness
as he lies on his bed.

He has set his foot on evil ways,
he clings to what is evil.

Your love, Lord, reaches to heaven;
your truth to the skies.
Your justice is like God's mountain,
your judgments like the deep.

To both man and beast you give protection.
O Lord, how precious is your love.
My God, the sons of men
find refuge in the shelter of your wings.

They feast on the riches of your house;
they drink from the stream of your delight.
In you is the source of life
and in your light we see light.

Keep on loving those who know you,
doing justice for upright hearts.
Let the foot of the proud not crush me
nor the hand of the wicked cast me out.

See how the evil-doers fall!
Flung down, they shall never arise.

Psalm-prayer

Lord, you are the source of unfailing light.
Give us true knowledge of your mercy so that we

may renounce our pride and be filled with the
riches of your house.

Ant. 2 **O God, you are great and glorious; we
marvel at your power.**

CANTICLE   *Judith 16:2–3a, 13–15*
God who created the world takes care of his
people

They were singing a new song (Revelation 5:9).

Strike up the instruments,
a song to my God with timbrels,
chant to the Lord with cymbals.
Sing to him a new song,
exalt and acclaim his name.

A new hymn I will sing to my God.
O Lord, great are you and glorious,
wonderful in power and unsurpassable.

Let your every creature serve you;
for you spoke, and they were made,
you sent forth your spirit, and they were
    created;
no one can resist your word.

The mountains to their bases, and the seas, are
    shaken;
the rocks, like wax, melt before your glance.

But to those who fear you,
you are very merciful.

Ant. 3   **Exult in God's presence with hymns of
praise.**

Psalm 47
The Lord Jesus is King of all

*He is seated at the right hand of the Father, and
his kingdom will have no end.*

All peoples, clap your hands,
cry to God with shouts of joy!
For the Lord, the Most High, we must fear,
great king over all the earth.

He subdues peoples under us
and nations under our feet.
Our inheritance, our glory, is from him,
given to Jacob out of love.

God goes up with shouts of joy;
the Lord goes up with trumpet blast.
Sing praise for God, sing praise,
sing praise to our king, sing praise.

God is king of all the earth.
Sing praise with all your skill.
God is king over the nations;
God reigns on his holy throne.

The princes of the peoples are assembled
with the people of Abraham's God.
The rulers of the earth belong to God,
to God who reigns over all.

Psalm-prayer

God, King of all peoples and all ages, it is your
victory we celebrate as we sing with all the skill
at our command. Help us always to overcome
evil by good, that we may rejoice in your triumph for ever.

READING   *Tobit 4:15a. 16a. 18a. 19*

Do to no one what you yourself dislike. Give to
the hungry some of your bread, and to the naked
some of your clothing. Seek counsel from every
wise man. At all times bless the Lord God, and
ask him to make all your paths straight and to
grant success to all your endeavors and plans.

RESPONSORY

Incline my heart according to your will, O God.
—Incline my heart according to your will, O
   God.
Speed my steps along your path,
—according to your will, O God.
Glory to the Father . . .
—Incline my heart . . .

CANTICLE OF ZECHARIAH

Ant.   Show us your mercy, Lord; remember your
        holy covenant.

INTERCESSIONS

Let us give thanks to Christ and offer him con-
    tinual praise, for he sanctifies us and calls us
    his brothers:
    Lord, help your brothers to grow in holiness.
With single-minded devotion we dedicate the
    beginnings of this day to the honor of your
    resurrection,
—may we make the whole day pleasing to you
    by our works of holiness.
As a sign of your love, you renew each day for
    the sake of our well-being and happiness,
—renew us daily for the sake of your glory.
Teach us today to recognize your presence in
    all men,
—especially in the poor and in those who
    mourn.
Grant that we may live today in peace with all
    men,
—never rendering evil for evil.

Our Father . . .

PRAYER

God our Savior,
hear our morning prayer:
help us to follow the light
and live the truth.
In you we have been born again
as sons and daughters of light:
may we be your witnesses before all the world.

We ask this through our Lord Jesus Christ,
   your Son,
who lives and reigns with you and the Holy
   Spirit,
one God, for ever and ever.

May the Lord bless us,
protect us from all evil
and bring us to everlasting life.
—Amen.

WEDNESDAY EVENING PRAYER

God, come to my assistance.
—Lord, make haste to help me.

Glory to the Father, and to the Son, and to the
  Holy Spirit:
as it was in the beginning, is now, and will be
  for ever. Amen. Alleluia.

PSALMODY

Ant. 1   The Lord is my light and my help; whom
         shall I fear?

Psalm 27
God stands by us in dangers
God now truly dwells with me (Revelation 21:3).

I

The Lord is my light and my help;
whom shall I fear?
The Lord is the stronghold of my life;
before whom shall I shrink?

When evil-doers draw near
to devour my flesh,—

it is they, my enemies and foes,
who stumble and fall.

Though an army encamp against me
my heart would not fear.

Though war break out against me
even then would I trust.

There is one thing I ask of the Lord,
for this I long,
to live in the house of the Lord,
all the days of my life,
to savor the sweetness of the Lord,
to behold his temple.

For there he keeps me safe in his tent
in the day of evil.
He hides me in the shelter of his tent,
on a rock he sets me safe.

And now my head shall be raised
above my foes who surround me
and I shall offer within his tent
a sacrifice of joy.

I will sing and make music for the Lord.

Ant. 2   I long to look on you, O Lord; do not turn
          your face from me.

II

*Some rose to present lies and false evidence
against Jesus* (Mark 14:57).

O Lord, hear my voice when I call;
have mercy and answer.

Of you my heart has spoken:
"Seek his face."

It is your face, O Lord, that I seek;
hide not your face.
Dismiss not your servant in anger;
you have been my help.

Do not abandon or forsake me,
O God my help!
Though father and mother forsake me,
the Lord will receive me.

Instruct me, Lord, in your way;
on an even path lead me.
When they lie in ambush protect me
from my enemy's greed.
False witnesses rise against me,
breathing out fury.

I am sure I shall see the Lord's goodness
in the land of the living.
Hope in him, hold firm and take heart.
Hope in the Lord!

Psalm-prayer

Father, you protect and strengthen those who
hope in you; you heard the cry of your Son and
kept him safe in your tent in the day of evil.
Grant that your servants who seek your face in

times of trouble may see your goodness in the
land of the living.

Ant. 3   He is the first-born of all creation; in
every way the primacy is his.

CANTICLE   *Colossians 1:12–20*
Christ the first-born of all creation and the first-
born from the dead

Let us give thanks to the Father
for having made you worthy
to share the lot of the saints
in light.

He rescued us
from the power of darkness
and brought us
into the kingdom of his beloved Son.
Through him we have redemption,
the forgiveness of our sins.

He is the image of the invisible God,
the first-born of all creatures.
In him everything in heaven and on earth was
    created,
things visible and invisible.

All were created through him;
all were created for him.
He is before all else that is.
In him everything continues in being.

It is he who is head of the body, the church!
he who is the beginning,
the first-born of the dead,
so that primacy may be his in everything.

It pleased God to make absolute fullness reside
   in him
and, by means of him, to reconcile everything
   in his person,
both on earth and in the heavens,
making peace through the blood of his cross.

READING   *James 1:19–25*

Keep this in mind, dear brothers. Let every
man be quick to hear, slow to speak, slow to
anger; for a man's anger does not fulfill God's
justice. Strip away all that is filthy, every vicious
excess. Humbly welcome the word that has
taken root in you, with its power to save you. Act
on this word. If all you do is listen to it, you are
deceiving yourselves.

A man who listens to God's word but does
not put it into practice is like a man who looks
into a mirror at the face he was born with: he
looks at himself, then goes off and promptly
forgets what he looked like. There is, on the
other hand, the man who peers into freedom's
ideal law and abides by it. He is no forgetful
listener, but one who carries out the law in

practice. Blest will this man be in whatever he does.

RESPONSORY

Claim me once more as your own, Lord, and have mercy on me.
—Claim me once more as your own, Lord, and have mercy on me.
Do not abandon me with the wicked;
—have mercy on me.
Glory to the Father . . .
—Claim me once . . .

CANTICLE OF MARY

Ant. The Almighty has done great things for me, and holy is his Name.

INTERCESSIONS

In all that we do, let the name of the Lord be praised, for he surrounds his chosen people with boundless love. Let our prayer rise up to him:
Lord, show us your love.
Remember your Church, Lord,
—keep her from every evil and let her grow to the fullness of your love.
Let the nations recognize you as the one true God,

—and Jesus your Son, as the Messiah whom
    you sent.
Grant prosperity to our neighbors,
—give them life and happiness for ever.
Console those who are burdened with oppres-
    sive work and daily hardships,
—preserve the dignity of workers.
Open wide the doors of your compassion to
    those who have died today,
—and in your mercy receive them into your
    kingdom.
Our Father . . .

PRAYER

Lord,
watch over us by day and by night.
In the midst of life's countless changes
strengthen us with your never-changing love.

We ask this through our Lord Jesus Christ,
    your Son,
who lives and reigns with you and the Holy
    Spirit,
one God, for ever and ever.

May the Lord bless us,
protect us from all evil
and bring us to everlasting life.
—Amen.

God, come to my assistance.
—Lord, make haste to help me.

Glory to the Father, and to the Son, and to the
   Holy Spirit:
as it was in the beginning, is now, and will be
   for ever. Amen. Alleluia.

Ant. 1   Awake, lyre and harp, with praise let us
         awake the dawn.

Psalm 57
Morning prayer in affliction

This psalm tells of our Lord's passion (Saint
Augustine).

Have mercy on me, God, have mercy
for in you my soul has taken refuge.
In the shadow of your wings I take refuge
till the storms of destruction pass by.

I call to God the Most High,
to God who has always been my help.
May he send from heaven and save me
and shame those who assail me.

May God send his truth and his love.

My soul lies down among lions,
who would devour the sons of men.
Their teeth are spears and arrows,
their tongue a sharpened sword.

O God, arise above the heavens;
may your glory shine on earth!

They laid a snare for my steps,
my soul was bowed down.
They dug a pit in my path
but fell in it themselves.

My heart is ready, O God,
my heart is ready.
I will sing, I will sing your praise.
Awake, my soul,
awake, lyre and harp,
I will awake the dawn.

I will thank you, Lord, among the peoples,
among the nations I will praise you—
for your love reaches to the heavens
and your truth to the skies.
O God, arise above the heavens;
may your glory shine on earth!

Psalm-prayer

Lord, send your mercy and your truth to rescue
us from the snares of the devil, and we will

praise you among the peoples and proclaim you
to the nations, happy to be known as companions
of your Son.

Ant. 2   My people, says the Lord, will be filled
          with my blessings.

CANTICLE   *Jeremiah 31:10–14*
   The happiness of a people who have been
                    redeemed

*Jesus was to die . . . to gather God's scattered
children into one fold* (John 11:51, 52).

Hear the word of the Lord, O nations,
proclaim it on distant coasts, and say:
He who scattered Israel, now gathers them to-
     gether,
he guards them as a shepherd his flock.

The Lord shall ransom Jacob,
he shall redeem him from the hand of his con-
     queror.
Shouting, they shall mount the heights of Zion,
they shall come streaming to the Lord's bless-
     ings:
the grain, the wine, and the oil,
the sheep and the oxen;
they themselves shall be like watered gardens,
never again shall they languish.

Then the virgins shall make merry and dance,
and young men and old as well.

I will turn their mourning into joy,
I will console and gladden them after their
    sorrows.
I will lavish choice portions upon the priests,
and my people shall be filled with my bless-
    ings,
says the Lord.

Ant. 3   The Lord is great and worthy to be
            praised in the city of our God.

Psalm 48
Thanksgiving for the people's deliverance

*He took me up a high mountain and showed me
Jerusalem, God's holy city* (Revelation 21:10).

The Lord is great and worthy to be praised
in the city of our God.
His holy mountain rises in beauty,
the joy of all the earth.

Mount Zion, true pole of the earth,
the Great King's city!
God, in the midst of its citadels,
has shown himself its stronghold.

For the kings assembled together,
together they advanced.

They saw; at once they were astounded;
dismayed, they fled in fear.

A trembling seized them there,
like the pangs of birth.
By the east wind you have destroyed
the ships of Tarshish.

As we have heard, so we have seen
in the city of our God,
in the city of the Lord of hosts
which God upholds for ever.

O God, we ponder your love
within your temple.
Your praise, O God, like your name
reaches to the ends of the earth.

With justice your right hand is filled.
Mount Zion rejoices;
the people of Judah rejoice
at the sight of your judgments.

Walk through Zion, walk all around it;
count the number of its towers.
Review all its ramparts,
examine its castles,

that you may tell the next generation
that such is our God,
our God for ever and always.
It is he who leads us.

Psalm-prayer

Father, the body of your risen Son is the temple not made by human hands and the defending wall of the new Jerusalem. May this holy city, built of living stones, shine with spiritual radiance and witness to your greatness in the sight of all nations.

READING   *Isaiah 66:1–2*

Thus says the Lord:
The heavens are my throne,
    and the earth is my footstool.
What kind of house can you build for me;
    what is to be my resting place?
My hand made all these things
    when all of them came to be, says the Lord.
This is the one whom I approve:
    the lowly and afflicted man who trembles at
    my word.

RESPONSORY

From the depths of my heart I cry to you; hear
    me, O Lord.
—From the depths of my heart I cry to you;
    hear me, O Lord.
I will do what you desire;
—hear me, O Lord.

Glory to the Father . . .
—From the depths . . .

CANTICLE OF ZECHARIAH

Ant. Let us serve the Lord in holiness, and he
will save us from our enemies.

INTERCESSIONS

The Lord Jesus Christ has given us the light of
another day. In return we thank him as we
cry out:
Lord, bless us and bring us close to you.
You offered yourself in sacrifice for our sins,
—accept our intentions and our work today.
You bring us joy by the light of another day,
—let the morning star rise in our hearts.
Give us strength to be patient with those we
meet today,
—and so imitate you.
Make us aware of your mercy this morning,
Lord,
—and let your strength be our delight.

Our Father . . .

PRAYER

All-powerful and ever-living God,
at morning, noon, and evening we pray:

cast out from our hearts the darkness of sin
and bring us to the light of your truth,
Jesus Christ, who lives and reigns with you
   and the Holy Spirit,
one God, for ever and ever.

May the Lord bless us,
protect us from all evil
and bring us to everlasting life.
—Amen.

THURSDAY EVENING PRAYER

God, come to my assistance.
—Lord, make haste to help me.

Glory to the Father, and to the Son, and to the
  Holy Spirit:
as it was in the beginning, is now, and will be
  for ever. Amen. Alleluia.

PSALMODY

Ant. 1   I cried to you, Lord, and you healed me;
         I will praise you for ever.

Psalm 30
Thanksgiving for deliverance from death

*Christ, risen in glory, gives continual thanks to
his Father* (Cassian).

I will praise you, Lord, you have rescued me
and have not let my enemies rejoice over
  me.

O Lord, I cried to you for help
and you, my God, have healed me.
O Lord, you have raised my soul from the dead,
restored me to life from those who sink into
  the grave.

Sing psalms to the Lord, you who love him,
give thanks to his holy name.

His anger lasts a moment; his favor through
    life.
At night there are tears, but joy comes with
    dawn.

I said to myself in my good fortune:
"Nothing will ever disturb me."
Your favor had set me on a mountain fastness,
then you hid your face and I was put to confu-
    sion.
To you, Lord, I cried,
to my God I made appeal:

"What profit would my death be, my going to
    the grave?
Can dust give you praise or proclaim your
    truth?"

The Lord listened and had pity.
The Lord came to my help.
For me you have changed my mourning into
    dancing,
you removed my sackcloth and clothed me
    with joy.
So my soul sings psalms to you unceasingly.
O Lord my God, I will thank you for ever.

Psalm-prayer

God our Father, glorious in giving life, and
even more glorious in restoring it, when his last

night on earth came, your Son shed tears of
blood, but dawn brought incomparable gladness.
Do not turn away from us, or we shall fall back
into dust, but rather turn our mourning into joy
by raising us up with Christ.

Ant. 2   The one who is sinless in the eyes of God
          is blessed indeed.

Psalm 32
They are happy whose sins are forgiven

*David speaks of the happiness of the man who
is holy in God's eyes not because of his own
worth, but because God has justified him* (Romans 4:6).

Happy the man whose offense is forgiven,
whose sin is remitted.
O happy the man to whom the Lord
imputes no guilt,
in whose spirit is no guile.

I kept it secret and my frame was wasted.
I groaned all the day long—
for night and day your hand
was heavy upon me.
Indeed, my strength was dried up
as by the summer's heat.

But now I have acknowledged my sins;
my guilt I did not hide.

I said: "I will confess
my offense to the Lord."
And you, Lord, have forgiven
the guilt of my sin.

So let every good man pray to you
in the time of need.
The floods of water may reach high
but him they shall not reach.
You are my hiding place, O Lord;
you save me from distress.
You surround me with cries of deliver-
    ance.

I will instruct you and teach you
the way you should go;
I will give you counsel
with my eye upon you.

Be not like horse and mule, unintelligent,
needing bridle and bit,
else they will not approach you.
Many sorrows has the wicked
but he who trusts in the Lord,
loving mercy surrounds him.

Rejoice, rejoice in the Lord,
exult, you just!
O come, ring out your joy,
all you upright of heart.

Psalm-prayer

You desired, Lord, to keep from us your indignation and so did not spare Jesus Christ, who
was wounded for our sins. We are your prodigal
children, but confessing our sins we come back
to you. Embrace us that we may rejoice in your
mercy together with Christ your beloved Son.

Ant. 3 The Father has given Christ all power,
honor and kingship; all people will obey
him.

CANTICLE *Revelation 11:17–18; 12:10b–12a*
The judgment of God

We praise you, the Lord God Almighty,
who is and who was.
You have assumed your great power,
you have begun your reign.

The nations have raged in anger,
but then came your day of wrath
and the moment to judge the dead:
the time to reward your servants the prophets
and the holy ones who revere you,
the great and the small alike.

Now have salvation and power come,
the reign of our God and the authority
of his Anointed One.

For the accuser of our brothers is cast out,
who night and day accused them before God.

They defeated him by the blood of the Lamb
and by the word of their testimony;
love for life did not deter them from death.
So rejoice, you heavens,
and you that dwell therein!

READING   *1 Peter 1:6–9*

There is cause for rejoicing here. You may for
a time have to suffer the distress of many trials;
but this is so that your faith, which is more precious than the passing splendor of fire-tried gold,
may by its genuineness lead to praise, glory, and
honor when Jesus Christ appears. Although you
have never seen him, you love him, and without
seeing you now believe in him, and rejoice with
inexpressible joy touched with glory because
you are achieving faith's goal, your salvation.

RESPONSORY

The Lord has given us food, bread of the finest
    wheat.
—The Lord has given us food, bread of the
    finest wheat.
Honey from the rock to our heart's content,
—bread of the finest wheat.

Glory to the Father . . .
—The Lord has . . .

CANTICLE OF MARY

Ant. God has cast down the mighty from their
thrones, and has lifted up the lowly.

INTERCESSIONS

Our hope is in God, who gives us help. Let us
call upon him, and say:
Look kindly on your children, Lord.
Lord, our God, you made an eternal covenant
with your people,
—keep us ever mindful of your mighty deeds.
Let your ordained ministers grow toward perfect love,
—and preserve your faithful people in unity by
the bond of peace.
Be with us in our work of building the earthly
city,
—that in building we may not labor in vain.
Send workers into your vineyard,
—and glorify your name among the nations.
Welcome into the company of your saints our
relatives and benefactors who have died,
—may we share their happiness one day.

PRAYER

Father,
you illumine the night
and bring the dawn to scatter darkness.
Let us pass this night in safety,
free from Satan's power,
and rise when morning comes
to give you thanks and praise.

We ask this through our Lord Jesus Christ,
    your Son,
who lives and reigns with you and the Holy
    Spirit,
one God, for ever and ever.

May the Lord bless us,
protect us from all evil
and bring us to everlasting life.
—Amen.

FRIDAY MORNING PRAYER

God, come to my assistance.
—Lord, make haste to help me.

Glory to the Father, and to the Son, and to the
    Holy Spirit:
as it was in the beginning, is now, and will be
    for ever. Amen. Alleluia.

PSALMODY

Ant. 1 Lord, you will accept the true sacrifice
        offered on your altar.

Psalm 51
O God, have mercy on me

*Your inmost being must be renewed, and you
must put on the new man* (Ephesians 4:23–24).

Have mercy on me, God, in your kindness.
In your compassion blot out my offense.
O wash me more and more from my guilt
and cleanse me from my sin.

My offenses truly I know them;
my sin is always before me.
Against you, you alone, have I sinned;
what is evil in your sight I have done.

That you may be justified when you give sen-
    tence

and be without reproach when you judge.
O see, in guilt I was born,
a sinner was I conceived.

Indeed you love truth in the heart;
then in the secret of my heart teach me wisdom.
O purify me, then I shall be clean;
O wash me, I shall be whiter than snow.

Make me hear rejoicing and gladness,
that the bones you have crushed may revive.
From my sins turn away your face
and blot out all my guilt.

A pure heart create for me, O God,
put a steadfast spirit within me.
Do not cast me away from your presence,
nor deprive me of your holy spirit.

Give me again the joy of your help;
with a spirit of fervor sustain me,
that I may teach transgressors your ways
and sinners may return to you.

O rescue me, God, my helper,
and my tongue shall ring out your goodness.
O Lord, open my lips
and my mouth shall declare your praise.

For in sacrifice you take no delight,
burnt offering from me you would refuse,

my sacrifice, a contrite spirit.
A humbled, contrite heart you will not spurn.

In your goodness, show favor to Zion:
rebuild the walls of Jerusalem.
Then you will be pleased with lawful sacrifice,
holocausts offered on your altar.

Psalm-prayer

Father, he who knew no sin was made sin for
us, to save us and restore us to your friendship.
Look upon our contrite heart and afflicted spirit
and heal our troubled conscience, so that in the
joy and strength of the Holy Spirit we may proclaim your praise and glory before all the nations.

Ant. 2   All the descendants of Israel will glory in
the Lord's gift of victory.

CANTICLE   *Isaiah 45:15–25*
People of all nations will become disciples of
the Lord

Every knee shall bend at the name of Jesus (Philippians 2:10).

Truly with you God is hidden,
the God of Israel, the savior!
Those are put to shame and disgrace

who vent their anger against him.
Those go in disgrace
who carve images.

Israel, you are saved by the Lord, saved
    forever!
You shall never be put to shame or disgrace
in future ages.

For thus says the Lord,
the creator of the heavens,
who is God,
the designer and maker of the earth
who established it,
not creating it to be a waste,
but designing it to be lived in:

I am the Lord, and there is no other.
I have not spoken from hiding
nor from some dark place of the earth.
And I have not said to the descendants of
    Jacob,
"Look for me in an empty waste."
I, the Lord, promise justice,
I foretell what is right.

Come and assemble, gather together,
you fugitives from among the Gentiles!
They are without knowledge who bear wooden
    idols
and pray to gods that cannot save.

Come here and declare
in counsel together:
Who announced this from the beginning
and foretold it from of old?
Was it not I, the Lord,
besides whom there is no other God?
There is no just and saving God but me.

Turn to me and be safe,
all you ends of the earth,
for I am God; there is no other!

By myself I swear,
uttering my just decree
and my unalterable word:

To me every knee shall bend;
by me every tongue shall swear,
saying, "Only in the Lord
are just deeds and power.

Before him in shame shall come
all who vent their anger against him.
In the Lord shall be the vindication and the
    glory
of all the descendants of Israel."

Ant. 3   Let us go into God's presence singing for
    joy.

Psalm 100
The joyful song of those entering God's
Temple

*The Lord calls his ransomed people to sing songs
of victory* (Saint Athanasius).

Cry out with joy to the Lord, all the earth.
Serve the Lord with gladness.
Come before him, singing for joy.

Know that he, the Lord, is God.
He made us, we belong to him,
we are his people, the sheep of his flock.

Go within his gates, giving thanks.
Enter his courts with songs of praise.
Give thanks to him and bless his name.

Indeed, how good is the Lord,
eternal his merciful love.
He is faithful from age to age.

Psalm-prayer

With joy and gladness we cry out to you, Lord,
and ask you: open our hearts to sing your praises
and announce your goodness and truth.

READING   *Ephesians 4:29–32*

Never let evil talk pass your lips; say only the
good things men need to hear, things that will

really help them. Do nothing that will sadden
the Holy Spirit with whom you were sealed
against the day of redemption. Get rid of all bit-
terness, all passion and anger, harsh words,
slander, and malice of every kind. In place of
these, be kind to one another, compassionate,
and mutually forgiving, just as God has forgiven
you in Christ.

RESPONSORY

At daybreak, be merciful to me.
—At daybreak, be merciful to me.
Make known to me the path that I must walk.
—Be merciful to me.
Glory to the Father . . .
—At daybreak, be . . .

CANTICLE OF ZECHARIAH

Ant. The Lord has come to his people and set
them free.

INTERCESSIONS

Through his cross the Lord Jesus brought salvation to the human race. We adore him and
in faith we call out to him:
Lord, pour out your mercy upon us.
Christ, Rising Sun, warm us with your rays,

—and restrain us from every evil impulse.
Keep guard over our thoughts, words and actions,
—and make us pleasing in your sight this day.
Turn your gaze from our sinfulness,
—and cleanse us from our iniquities.
Through your cross and resurrection,
—fill us with the consolation of the Spirit.
Our Father . . .

PRAYER

God our Father,
you conquer the darkness of ignorance
by the light of your Word.
Strengthen within our hearts
the faith you have given us;
let not temptation ever quench the fire
that your love has kindled within us.

We ask this through our Lord Jesus Christ,
your Son,
who lives and reigns with you and the Holy
Spirit,
one God, for ever and ever.

May the Lord bless us,
protect us from all evil
and bring us to everlasting life.
—Amen.

FRIDAY EVENING PRAYER

God, come to my assistance.
—Lord, make haste to help me.

Glory to the Father, and to the Son, and to the
   Holy Spirit:
as it was in the beginning, is now, and will be
   for ever. Amen. Alleluia.

PSALMODY

Ant. 1   Lord, lay your healing hand upon me, for
         I have sinned.

Psalm 41
Prayer of a sick person

*One of you will betray me, yes, one who eats
with me* (Mark 14:18).

Happy the man who considers the poor and
   the weak.
The Lord will save him in the day of evil,
will guard him, give him life, make him happy
   in the land—

and will not give him up to the will of his foes.
The Lord will help him on his bed of pain,
he will bring him back from sickness to
   health.

As for me, I said: "Lord, have mercy on me,
heal my soul for I have sinned against you."

My foes are speaking evil against me.
"How long before he dies and his name be for-
     gotten?"
They come to visit me and speak empty words,
their hearts full of malice, they spread it
     abroad.

My enemies whisper together against me.
They all weigh up the evil which is on me:
"Some deadly thing has fastened upon him,
he will not rise again from where he lies."
Thus even my friend, in whom I trusted,
who ate my bread, has turned against me.

But you, O Lord, have mercy on me.
Let me rise once more and I will repay them.
By this I shall know that you are my friend,
if my foes do not shout in triumph over me.
If you uphold me I shall be unharmed
and set in your presence for evermore.

Blessed be the Lord, the God of Israel
from age to age. Amen.

Psalm-prayer

Lord Jesus, healer of soul and body, you said:
Blessed are the merciful, they will obtain mercy.
Teach us to come to the aid of the needy in a
spirit of brotherly love, that we in turn may be
received and strengthened by you.

Ant. 2   **The mighty Lord is with us; the God of Jacob is our stronghold.**

Psalm 46
God our refuge and strength

He shall be called Emmanuel, which means: God-with-us (Matthew 1:23).

God is for us a refuge and strength,
a helper close at hand, in time of distress:
so we shall not fear though the earth should rock,
though the mountains fall into the depths of the sea,
even though its waters rage and foam,
even though the mountains be shaken by its waves.

The Lord of hosts is with us:
the God of Jacob is our stronghold.

The waters of a river give joy to God's city,
the holy place where the Most High dwells.
God is within, it cannot be shaken;
God will help it at the dawning of the day.
Nations are in tumult, kingdoms are shaken:
he lifts his voice, the earth shrinks away.

The Lord of hosts is with us:
the God of Jacob is our stronghold.

Come, consider the works of the Lord,
the redoubtable deeds he has done on the
    earth.
He puts an end to wars over all the earth;
the bow he breaks, the spear he snaps.
He burns the shields with fire.
"Be still and know that I am God,
supreme among the nations, supreme on the
    earth!"

The Lord of hosts is with us:
the God of Jacob is our stronghold.

Psalm-prayer

All-powerful Father, the refuge and strength
of your people, you protect in adversity and de-
fend in prosperity those who put their trust in
you. May they persevere in seeking your will and
find their way to you through obedience.—

Ant. 3   All nations will come and worship be-
          fore you, O Lord.

CANTICLE   *Revelation 15:3–4*
                Hymn of adoration

Mighty and wonderful are your works,
Lord God Almighty!
Righteous and true are your ways,
O King of the nations!

Who would dare refuse you honor,
or the glory due your name, O Lord?

Since you alone are holy,
all nations shall come
and worship in your presence.
Your mighty deeds are clearly seen.

READING *Romans 15:1–6*

We who are strong in faith should be patient
with the scruples of those whose faith is weak;
we must not be selfish. Each should please his
neighbor so as to do him good by building up his
spirit. Thus, in accord with Scripture, Christ did
not please himself: "The reproaches they uttered
against you fell on me." Everything written before our time was written for our instruction,
that we might derive hope from the lessons of
patience and the words of encouragement in the
Scriptures. May God, the source of all patience
and encouragement, enable you to live in perfect
harmony with one another according to the
spirit of Christ Jesus, so that with one heart and
voice you may glorify God, the Father of our
Lord Jesus Christ.

RESPONSORY

Christ loved us and washed away our sins, in
his own blood.

—Christ loved us and washed away our sins, in
his own blood.
He made us a nation of kings and priests,
—in his own blood.
Glory to the Father . . .
—Christ loved us . . .

CANTICLE OF MARY

Ant. The Lord has come to the help of his servants, for he has remembered his promise
of mercy.

INTERCESSIONS

Blessed be God, who hears the prayers of the
needy, and fills the hungry with good things.
Let us pray to him in confidence:
Lord, show us your mercy.
Merciful Father, upon the cross Jesus offered
you the perfect evening sacrifice,
—we pray now for all the suffering members
of his Church.
Release those in bondage, give sight to the
blind,
—shelter the widow and the orphan.
Clothe your faithful people in the armor of
salvation,
—and shield them from the deceptions of the
devil.

Let your merciful presence be with us, Lord, at
   the hour of our death,
—may we be found faithful and leave this
   world in your peace.

Lead the departed into the light of your dwelling place,
—that they may gaze upon you for all eternity.

Our Father . . .

PRAYER

God our Father,
help us to follow the example
of your Son's patience in suffering.
By sharing the burden he carries,
may we come to share his glory
in the kingdom where he lives with you and
   the Holy Spirit,
one God, for ever and ever.

May the Lord bless us,
protect us from all evil
and bring us to everlasting life.
—Amen.

SATURDAY MORNING PRAYER

God, come to my assistance.
—Lord, make haste to help me.

Glory to the Father, and to the Son, and to the
    Holy Spirit:
as it was in the beginning, is now, and will be
    for ever. Amen. Alleluia.

Ant. 1   Dawn finds me ready to welcome you,
            my God.

Psalm 119:145–152

I call with all my heart; Lord, hear me,
I will keep your commands.
I call upon you, save me
and I will do your will.

I rise before dawn and cry for help,
I hope in your word.
My eyes watch through the night
to ponder your promise.

In your love hear my voice, O Lord;
give me life by your decrees.
Those who harm me unjustly draw near:
they are far from your law.

But you, O Lord, are close:
your commands are truth.
Long have I known that your will
is established for ever.

Psalm-prayer

Save us by the power of your hand, Father, for our enemies have ignored your words. May the fire of your word consume our sins, and its brightness illumine our hearts.

Ant. 2   The Lord is my strength, and I shall sing his praise, for he has become my savior.

CANTICLE   *Exodus 15:1–4a, 8–13, 17–18*
Hymn of victory after the crossing of the Red Sea

Those who had conquered the beast were singing the song of Moses, God's servant (Revelation 15: 2–3).

I will sing to the Lord, for he is gloriously triumphant;
horse and chariot he has cast into the sea.

My strength and my courage is the Lord,
and he has been my savior.
He is my God, I praise him;
the God of my father, I extol him.

The Lord is a warrior,
Lord is his name!
Pharaoh's chariots and army he hurled into
   the sea.

At a breath of your anger the waters piled up,
the flowing waters stood like a mound,
the flood waters congealed in the midst of the
   sea.

The enemy boasted, "I will pursue and over-
   take them;
I will divide the spoils and have my fill of
   them;
I will draw my sword; my hand shall despoil
   them!"
When your wind blew, the sea covered them;
like lead they sank in the mighty waters.

Who is like to you among the gods, O Lord?
Who is like to you, magnificent in holiness?
O terrible in renown, worker of wonders,
when you stretched out your right hand, the
   earth swallowed them!

In your mercy you led the people you redeemed;
in your strength you guided them to your holy
   dwelling.
And you brought them in and planted them on

the mountain of your inheritance—
the place where you made your seat, O Lord,
the sanctuary, O Lord, which your hands established.
The Lord shall reign forever and ever.

Ant. 3   O praise the Lord, all you nations.

Psalm 117
Praise for God's loving compassion

*I affirm that . . . the Gentile peoples are to praise
God because of his mercy* (Romans 15:8–9).

O praise the Lord, all you nations,
acclaim him, all you peoples!

Strong is his love for us;
he is faithful for ever.

Psalm-prayer

God our Father, may all nations and peoples
praise you. May Jesus, who is called faithful and
true and who lives with you eternally, possess
our hearts for ever.

READING   *2 Peter 1:10–11*

Be solicitous to make your call and election
permanent, brothers; surely those who do so will
never be lost. On the contrary, your entry into the

everlasting kingdom of our Lord and Savior Jesus Christ will be richly provided for.

RESPONSORY

I cry to you, O Lord, for you are my refuge.
—I cry to you, O Lord, for you are my refuge.
You are all I desire in the land of the living;
—for you are my refuge.
Glory to the Father . . .
—I cry to . . .

CANTICLE OF ZECHARIAH

Ant.   Lord, shine on those who dwell in darkness and the shadow of death.

INTERCESSIONS

Let us all praise Christ. In order to become our faithful and merciful high priest before the Father's throne, he chose to become one of us, a brother in all things. In prayer we ask of him:
Lord, share with us the treasure of your love.
Sun of Justice, you filled us with light at our baptism,
—we dedicate this day to you.
At every hour of the day, we give you glory,
—in all our deeds, we offer you praise.

Mary, your mother, was obedient to your word,
—direct our lives in accordance with that word.
Our lives are surrounded with passing things; set our hearts on things of heaven,
—so that through faith, hope and charity we may come to enjoy the vision of your glory.

Our Father . . .

PRAYER

Lord,
free us from the dark night of death.
Let the light of resurrection
dawn within our hearts
to bring us to the radiance of eternal life.

We ask this through our Lord Jesus Christ, your Son,
who lives and reigns with you and the Holy Spirit,
one God, for ever and ever.

May the Lord bless us,
protect us from all evil
and bring us to everlasting life.
—Amen.

SATURDAY EVENING PRAYER

God, come to my assistance.
—Lord, make haste to help me.

Glory to the Father, and to the Son, and to the
Holy Spirit:
as it was in the beginning, is now, and will be
for ever. Amen. Alleluia.

PSALMODY

Ant. 1 Like burning incense, Lord, let my
prayer rise up to you.

Psalm 141:1–9
A prayer when in danger

*An angel stood before the face of God, thurible in
hand. The fragrant incense soaring aloft was
the prayer of God's people on earth* (Revelation
8:4).

I have called to you, Lord; hasten to help me!
Hear my voice when I cry to you.
Let my prayer arise before you like incense,
the raising of my hands like an evening obla-
tion.

Set, O Lord, a guard over my mouth;
keep watch at the door of my lips!
Do not turn my heart to things that are wrong,
to evil deeds with men who are sinners.

Never allow me to share in their feasting.
If a good man strikes or reproves me it is kindness;
but let the oil of the wicked not anoint my
head.
Let my prayer be ever against their malice.

Their princes were thrown down by the side of
the rock:
then they understood that my words were
kind.
As a millstone is shattered to pieces on the
ground,
so their bones were strewn at the mouth of the
grave.

To you, Lord God, my eyes are turned:
in you I take refuge; spare my soul!
From the trap they have laid for me keep me
safe:
keep me from the snares of those who do evil.

Psalm-prayer

Lord, from the rising of the sun to its setting
your name is worthy of all praise. Let our prayer
come like incense before you. May the lifting up
of our hands be as an evening sacrifice acceptable to you, Lord our God.

Ant. 2   You are my refuge, Lord; you are all that
         I desire in life.

Psalm 142
You, Lord, are my refuge

*What is written in this psalm was fulfilled in
our Lord's passion* (Saint Hilary).

With all my voice I cry to the Lord,
with all my voice I entreat the Lord.
I pour out my troubles before him;
I tell him all my distress
while my spirit faints within me.
But you, O Lord, know my path.

On the way where I shall walk
they have hidden a snare to entrap me.
Look on my right and see:
there is not one who takes my part.
I have no means of escape,
not one who cares for my soul.

I cry to you, O Lord.
I have said: "You are my refuge,
all I have left in the land of the living."
Listen then to my cry
for I am in the depths of distress.

Rescue me from those who pursue me
for they are stronger than I.

Bring my soul out of this prison
and then I shall praise your name.
Around me the just will assemble
because of your goodness to me.

Psalm-prayer

Lord, we humbly ask for your goodness. May
you help us to hope in you, and give us a share
with your chosen ones in the land of the living.

Ant. 3   The Lord Jesus humbled himself, and
           God exalted him for ever.

CANTICLE   *Philippians 2:6–11*
         Christ, God's holy servant

Though he was in the form of God,
Jesus did not deem equality with God
something to be grasped at.

Rather, he emptied himself
and took the form of a slave,
being born in the likeness of men.

He was known to be of human estate,
and it was thus that he humbled himself,—
obediently accepting even death,
death on a cross!

Because of this,
God highly exalted him

and bestowed on him the name
above every other name,

So that at Jesus' name
every knee must bend
in the heavens, on the earth,
and under the earth,
and every tongue proclaim
to the glory of God the Father:
JESUS CHRIST IS LORD!

READING   *Romans 11:25, 30–36*

Brothers, I do not want you to be ignorant of this mystery lest you be conceited. Just as you were once disobedient to God and now have received mercy through their disobedience, so the Jews have become disobedient—since God wished to show you mercy—that they too may receive mercy. God has imprisoned all in disobedience that he might have mercy on all.

How deep are the riches and the wisdom and the knowledge of God! How inscrutable his judgments, how unsearchable his ways! For "who has known the mind of the Lord? Or who has been his counselor? Who has given him anything so as to deserve return?" For from him and through him and for him all things are. To him be glory forever. Amen.

RESPONSORY

Our hearts are filled with wonder as we contemplate your works, O Lord.
—Our hearts are filled with wonder as we contemplate your works, O Lord.
We praise the wisdom which wrought them
all,
—as we contemplate your works, O Lord.
Glory to the Father . . .
—Our hearts are filled with wonder as we contemplate your works, O Lord.

CANTICLE OF MARY

Ant.   Go, preach the good news of the kingdom;
freely you have received, freely give, alleluia.

INTERCESSIONS

We give glory to the one God—Father, Son and
Holy Spirit—and in our weakness we pray:
Lord, be with your people.
Holy Lord, Father all-powerful, let justice
spring up on the earth,
—then your people will dwell in the beauty of
peace.
Let every nation come into your kingdom,
—so that all peoples will be saved.

Let married couples live in your peace,
—and grow in mutual love.
Reward all who have done good to us, Lord,
—and grant them eternal life.
Lord, you attend the dying with great mercy,
—grant them an eternal dwelling.

Our Father . . .

PRAYER

Almighty God,
our hope and our strength,
without you we falter.
Help us to follow Christ
and to live according to your will.
We ask this through our Lord Jesus Christ,
    your Son,
who lives and reigns with you and the Holy
    Spirit,
one God, for ever and ever.

May the Lord bless us,
protect us from all evil
and bring us to everlasting life.
—Amen.

In Honor of the Blessed Virgin Mary

. . . hail, holy Mother . . .

THIS SECTION MAY BE PRAYED
ON FEASTS OF MARY

MORNING PRAYER

God, come to my assistance.
—Lord, make haste to help me.

Glory to the Father, and to the Son, and to the
Holy Spirit:
as it was in the beginning, is now, and will be
for ever. Amen. Alleluia.

PSALMODY

Ant. 1   Blessed are you, O Mary, for the world's
salvation came forth from you; now in
glory, you rejoice for ever with the Lord.
Intercede for us with your Son (alleluia).

Psalm 63:2–9
A soul thirsting for God

*Whoever has left the darkness of sin yearns for
God.*

O God, you are my God, for you I long;
for you my soul is thirsting.
My body pines for you
like a dry, weary land without water.
So I gaze on you in the sanctuary
to see your strength and your glory.

For your love is better than life,
my lips will speak your praise.

So I will bless you all my life,
in your name I will lift up my hands.
My soul shall be filled as with a banquet,
my mouth shall praise you with joy.

On my bed I remember you.
On you I muse through the night
for you have been my help;
in the shadow of your wings I rejoice.
My soul clings to you;
your right hand holds me fast.

Ant. 2   You are the glory of Jerusalem, the joy of
Israel; you are the fairest honor of our
race (Alleluia).

CANTICLE   *Daniel 3:57–88, 56*
Let all creatures praise the Lord

All you servants of the Lord, sing praise to him
(Revelation 19:5).

Bless the Lord, all you works of the Lord.
Praise and exalt him above all forever.
Angels of the Lord, bless the Lord.
You heavens, bless the Lord.
All you waters above the heavens, bless the
Lord.
All you hosts of the Lord, bless the Lord.
Sun and moon, bless the Lord.
Stars of heaven, bless the Lord.

Every shower and dew, bless the Lord.
All you winds, bless the Lord.
Fire and heat, bless the Lord.
Cold and chill, bless the Lord.
Dew and rain, bless the Lord.
Frost and chill, bless the Lord.
Ice and snow, bless the Lord.
Nights and days, bless the Lord.
Light and darkness, bless the Lord.
Lightnings and clouds, bless the Lord.

Let the earth bless the Lord.
Praise and exalt him above all forever.
Mountains and hills, bless the Lord.
Everything growing from the earth, bless the
    Lord.
You springs, bless the Lord.
Seas and rivers, bless the Lord.
You dolphins and all water creatures, bless the
    Lord.
All you birds of the air, bless the Lord.

All you beasts, wild and tame, bless the Lord.
You sons of men, bless the Lord.

O Israel, bless the Lord.
Praise and exalt him above all forever.
Priests of the Lord, bless the Lord.
Servants of the Lord, bless the Lord.
Spirits and souls of the just, bless the Lord.

Holy men of humble heart, bless the Lord.
Hananiah, Azariah, Mishael, bless the Lord.
Praise and exalt him above all forever.

Let us bless the Father, and the Son, and the
  Holy Spirit.
Let us praise and exalt him above all forever.
Blessed are you, Lord, in the firmament of
  heaven.
Praiseworthy and glorious and exalted above
  all forever.

Ant. 3 O Virgin Mary, how great your cause for
        joy; God found you worthy to bear Christ
        our Savior (Alleluia).

Psalm 149
The joy of God's holy people

*Let the sons of the Church, the children of the
new people, rejoice in Christ, their King* (Hesychius).

Sing a new song to the Lord,
his praise in the assembly of the faithful.
Let Israel rejoice in its Maker,

let Zion's sons exult in their king.
Let them praise his name with dancing
and make music with timbrel and harp.

For the Lord takes delight in his people.
He crowns the poor with salvation.
Let the faithful rejoice in their glory.
shout for joy and take their rest.
Let the praise of God be on their lips
and a two-edged sword in their hand,

to deal out vengeance to the nations
and punishment on all the peoples;
to bind their kings in chains
and their nobles in fetters of iron;
to carry out the sentence pre-ordained:
this honor is for all his faithful.

READING   *Isaiah 61:10*

I rejoice heartily in the Lord, in my God is the
    joy of my soul;
For he has clothed me with a robe of salvation,
    and wrapped me in a mantle of justice, like
    a bride bedecked with her jewels.

RESPONSORY

The Lord has chosen her,
his loved one from the beginning (alleluia, al-
    leluia).
—The Lord has chosen her,
his loved one from the beginning (alleluia, al-
    leluia).

He has taken her to live with him,
—his loved one from the beginning.
(—alleluia, alleluia.)
Glory to the Father . . .
—The Lord has . . .

CANTICLE OF ZECHARIAH

Ant.   Eve shut all her children out of Paradise;
the Virgin Mary opened wide its gates (Alleluia).

INTERCESSIONS

Let us glorify our Savior, who chose the Virgin
Mary for his mother. Let us ask him:
May your mother intercede for us, Lord.
Savior of the world, by your redeeming might
you preserved your mother beforehand from
all stain of sin,
—keep watch over us, lest we sin.
You are our redeemer, who made the immacu-
late Virgin Mary your purest home and the
sanctuary of the Holy Spirit,
—make us temples of your Spirit for ever.
Eternal Word, you taught your mother to
choose the better part,
—grant that in imitating her we might seek
the food that brings life everlasting.

King of kings, you lifted up your mother, body
  and soul, into heaven;
—help us to fix our thoughts on things above.
Lord of heaven and earth, you crowned Mary
  and set her at your right hand as queen,
—make us worthy to share this glory.

Our Father . . .

PRAYER

Lord God,
give to your people the joy
of continual health in mind and body.
With the prayers of the Virgin Mary to help us,
guide us through the sorrows of this life
to eternal happiness in the life to come.

Grant this through our Lord Jesus Christ, your
  Son,
who lives and reigns with you and the Holy
  Spirit,
one God, for ever and ever.

May the Lord bless us,
protect us from all evil
and bring us to everlasting life.
—Amen.

EVENING PRAYER

God, come to my assistance.
—Lord, make haste to help me.

Glory to the Father, and to the Son, and to the
   Holy Spirit:
as it was in the beginning, is now, and will be
   for ever. Amen. Alleluia.

Ant. 1   Hail, Mary, full of grace, the Lord is with
         you (alleluia).

Psalm 122

I rejoiced when I heard them say:
"Let us go to God's house."
And now our feet are standing
within your gates, O Jerusalem.

Jerusalem is built as a city
strongly compact.
It is there that the tribes go up,
the tribes of the Lord.

For Israel's law it is,
there to praise the Lord's name.
There were set the thrones of judgment
of the house of David.

For the peace of Jerusalem pray:
"Peace be to your homes!
May peace reign in your walls,
in your palaces, peace!"

For love of my brethren and friends
I say: "Peace upon you!"
For love of the house of the Lord
I will ask for your good.

Ant. 2   I am the handmaid of the Lord. Let it be
done to me as you have said (alleluia).

Psalm 127

If the Lord does not build the house,
in vain do its builders labor;
if the Lord does not watch over the city,
in vain does the watchman keep vigil.

In vain is your earlier rising,
your going later to rest,
you who toil for the bread you eat:
when he pours gifts on his beloved while they
slumber.

Truly sons are a gift from the Lord,
a blessing, the fruit of the womb.
Indeed the sons of youth
are like arrows in the hand of a warrior.

O the happiness of the man
who has filled his quiver with these arrows!
He will have no cause for shame
when he disputes with his foes in the gate-
ways.

Ant. 3 Blessed are you among women, and
blessed is the fruit of your womb (alleluia).

CANTICLE   *Ephesians 1:3–10*

Praised be the God and Father
of our Lord Jesus Christ,
who bestowed on us in Christ
every spiritual blessing in the heavens.

God chose us in him
before the world began,
to be holy
and blameless in his sight.

He predestined us
to be his adopted sons through Jesus Christ,
such was his will and pleasure,—

that all might praise the glorious favor
he has bestowed on us in his beloved.

In him and through his blood, we have been
redeemed,

and our sins forgiven,
so immeasurably generous
is God's favor to us.

God has given us the wisdom
to understand fully the mystery,
the plan he was pleased
to decree in Christ.

A plan to be carried out
in Christ, in the fullness of time,
to bring all things into one in him,
in the heavens and on the earth.

READING   *Galatians 4:4–5*

When the designated time had come, God sent
forth his Son born of a woman, born under the
law, to deliver from the law those who were sub-
jected to it, so that we might receive our status as
adopted sons.

RESPONSORY

Hail, Mary, full of grace, the Lord is with you
    (alleluia, alleluia).
—Hail, Mary, full of grace, the Lord is with you
    (alleluia).
Blessed are you among women, and blessed is
    the fruit of your womb.
—The Lord is with you.

(—Alleluia, alleluia.)
Glory to the Father . . .
—Hail, Mary, full . . .

CANTICLE OF MARY

Ant. Blessed are you, O Virgin Mary, for your
       great faith; all that the Lord promised
       you will come to pass through you (al-
       leluia).

INTERCESSIONS

Let us praise God our almighty Father, who
wished that Mary, his Son's mother, be celebrated by each generation. Now in need we
ask:
Mary, full of grace, intercede for us.
O God, worker of miracles, you made the im-
maculate Virgin Mary share body and soul
in your Son's glory in heaven,
—direct the hearts of your children to that
same glory.
You made Mary our mother. Through her in-
tercession grant strength to the weak, comfort to the sorrowing, pardon to sinners,
—salvation and peace to all.
You made Mary full of grace,
—grant all men the joyful abundance of your
grace.

Make your Church of one mind and one heart
   in love,
—and help all those who believe to be one in
   prayer with Mary, the mother of Jesus.
You crowned Mary queen of heaven,
—may all the dead rejoice in your kingdom
   with the saints for ever.

Our Father . . .

PRAYER

God our Father,
you gave the Holy Spirit to your apostles
as they joined in prayer with Mary, the mother
   of Jesus.
By the help of her prayers
keep us faithful in your service
and let our words and actions be so inspired
as to bring glory to your name.

Grant this through our Lord Jesus Christ, your
   Son,
who lives and reigns with you and the Holy
   Spirit,
one God, for ever and ever.

May the Lord bless us,
protect us from all evil
and bring us to everlasting life.
—Amen.

For the Dead

. . . give them eternal rest, O Lord . . .

THIS SECTION MAY BE PRAYED FOR THE DEAD

MORNING PRAYER

God, come to my assistance.
—Lord, make haste to help me.

Glory to the Father, and to the Son, and to the
 Holy Spirit:
as it was in the beginning, is now, and will be
 for ever. Amen. Alleluia.

Ant. 1   The bones that were crushed shall leap
         for joy before the Lord.

Psalm 51

Have mercy on me, God, in your kindness.
In your compassion blot out my offense.
O wash me more and more from my guilt
and cleanse me from my sin.

My offenses truly I know them;
my sin is always before me.
Against you, you alone, have I sinned;
what is evil in your sight I have done.

That you may be justified when you give sentence
and be without reproach when you judge,
O see, in guilt I was born,
a sinner was I conceived.

Indeed you love truth in the heart;
then in the secret of my heart teach me wisdom.
O purify me, then I shall be clean;
O wash me, I shall be whiter than snow.

Make me hear rejoicing and gladness,
that the bones you have crushed may revive.
From my sins turn away your face
and blot out all my guilt.

A pure heart create for me, O God,
put a steadfast spirit within me.
Do not cast me away from your presence,
nor deprive me of your holy spirit.

Give me again the joy of your help;
with a spirit of fervor sustain me,
that I may teach transgressors your ways
and sinners may return to you.

O rescue me, God, my helper,
and my tongue shall ring out your goodness.
O Lord, open my lips
and my mouth shall declare your praise.

For in sacrifice you take no delight,
burnt offering from me you would refuse,
my sacrifice, a contrite spirit.
A humbled, contrite heart you will not spurn.

In your goodness, show favor to Zion:
rebuild the walls of Jerusalem.
Then you will be pleased with lawful sacrifice,
holocausts offered on your altar.

Ant. 2   At the very threshold of death, rescue
me, Lord.

CANTICLE   *Isaiah 38:10–14, 17–20*

Once I said,
"In the noontime of life I must depart!
To the gates of the nether world I shall be con-
signed
for the rest of my years."

I said, "I shall see the Lord no more
in the land of the living.
No longer shall I behold my fellow men
among those who dwell in the world."

My dwelling, like a shepherd's tent,
is struck down and borne away from me;
you have folded up my life, like a weaver
who severs the last thread.

Day and night you give me over to torment;
I cry out until the dawn.
Like a lion he breaks all my bones;
day and night you give me over to torment.

Like a swallow I utter shrill cries;
I moan like a dove.
My eyes grow weak, gazing heaven-ward:
O Lord, I am in straits; be my surety!

You have preserved my life
from the pit of destruction,
when you cast behind your back
all my sins.

For it is not the nether world that gives you
     thanks,
nor death that praises you;
neither do those who go down into the pit
await your kindness.

The living, the living give you thanks,
as I do today.
Fathers declare to their sons,
O God, your faithfulness.

The Lord is our savior;
we shall sing to stringed instruments
in the house of the Lord
all the days of our life.

Ant. 3   I will praise my God all the days of my
            life.

Psalm 146

My soul, give praise to the Lord;
I will praise the Lord all my days,
make music to my God while I live.

Put no trust in princes,
in mortal men in whom there is no help.
Take their breath, they return to clay
and their plans that day come to nothing.

He is happy who is helped by Jacob's God,
whose hope is in the Lord his God,
who alone made heaven and earth,
the seas and all they contain.

It is he who keeps faith for ever,
who is just to those who are oppressed.
It is he who gives bread to the hungry,
the Lord, who sets prisoners free,

the Lord, who gives sight to the blind,
who raises up those who are bowed down,
the Lord, who protects the stranger
and upholds the widow and orphan.

It is the Lord who loves the just
but thwarts the path of the wicked.
The Lord will reign for ever,
Zion's God, from age to age.

READING   *1 Thessalonians 4:14*

If we believe that Jesus died and rose, God will bring forth with him from the dead those also who have fallen asleep believing in him.

RESPONSORY

I will praise you, Lord, for you have rescued me.
—I will praise you, Lord, for you have rescued me.
You turned my sorrow into joy,
—for you have rescued me.
Glory to the Father . . .
—I will praise . . .

CANTICLE OF ZECHARIAH

Ant.   I am the Resurrection, I am the Life; to believe in me means life, in spite of death, and all who believe and live in me shall never die.

INTERCESSIONS

Let us pray to the all-powerful Father who raised Jesus from the dead and gives new life to our mortal bodies, and say to him:
Lord, give us new life in Christ.
Father, through baptism we have been buried

with your Son and have risen with him in his resurrection,

—grant that we may walk in newness of life so that when we die, we may live with Christ for ever.

Provident Father, you have given us the living bread that has come down from heaven and which should always be eaten worthily,

—grant that we may eat this bread worthily and be raised up to eternal life on the last day.

Lord, you sent an angel to comfort your Son in his agony,

—give us the hope of your consolation when death draws near.

You delivered the three youths from the fiery furnace,

—free your faithful ones from the punishment they suffer for their sins.

God of the living and the dead, you raised Jesus from the dead,

—raise up those who have died and grant that we may share eternal glory with them.

Our Father . . .

PRAYER

Lord, hear our prayers.
By raising your Son from the dead, you have
   given us faith.
Strengthen our hope that N., our brother (sister),
will share in his resurrection.

We ask this through our Lord Jesus Christ,
   your Son,
who lives and reigns with you and the Holy
   Spirit,
one God, for ever and ever.

May the Lord bless us,
protect us from all evil
and bring us to everlasting life.
—Amen.

EVENING PRAYER

God, come to my assistance.
—Lord, make haste to help me.

Glory to the Father, and to the Son, and to the
  Holy Spirit:
as it was in the beginning, is now, and will be
  for ever. Amen. Alleluia.

Ant. 1   The Lord will keep you from all evil. He
         will guard your soul.

Psalm 121

I lift up my eyes to the mountains:
from where shall come my help?
My help shall come from the Lord
who made heaven and earth.

May he never allow you to stumble!
Let him sleep not, your guard.
No, he sleeps not nor slumbers,
Israel's guard.

The Lord is your guard and your shade;
at your right side he stands.
By day the sun shall not smite you
nor the moon in the night.

The Lord will guard you from evil,
he will guard your soul.
The Lord will guard your going and coming
both now and for ever.

Ant. 2　If you kept a record of our sins, Lord, who
　　　　could escape condemnation?

Psalm 130

Out of the depths I cry to you, O Lord,
Lord, hear my voice!
O let your ears be attentive
to the voice of my pleading.

If you, O Lord, should mark our guilt,
Lord, who would survive?
But with you is found forgiveness:
for this we revere you.

My soul is waiting for the Lord,
I count on his word.
My soul is longing for the Lord
more than watchman for daybreak.
Let the watchman count on daybreak
and Israel on the Lord.

Because with the Lord there is mercy
and fullness of redemption,
Israel indeed he will redeem
from all its iniquity.

Ant. 3   As the Father raises the dead and gives
         them life, so the Son gives life to whom
         he wills.

CANTICLE   *Philippians 2:6–11*

Though he was in the form of God,
Jesus did not deem equality with God
something to be grasped at.

Rather, he emptied himself
and took the form of a slave,
being born in the likeness of men.

He was known to be of human estate,
and it was thus that he humbled himself,
obediently accepting even death,
death on a cross!

Because of this,
God highly exalted him
and bestowed on him the name
above every other name,

so that at Jesus' name
every knee must bend
in the heavens, on the earth,
and under the earth,
and every tongue proclaim
to the glory of God the Father:
JESUS CHRIST IS LORD!

READING   *1 Corinthians 15:55–57*

O death, where is your victory? O death, where is your sting? But thanks be to God who has given us the victory through our Lord Jesus Christ.

RESPONSORY

In you, Lord, is our hope. We shall never hope in vain.
—In you, Lord, is our hope. We shall never hope in vain.
We shall dance and rejoice in your mercy.
—We shall never hope in vain.
Glory to the Father . . .
—In you, Lord . . .

CANTICLE OF MARY

Ant.   All that the Father gives me will come to me, and who ever comes to me I shall not turn away.

INTERCESSIONS

We acknowledge Christ the Lord through whom we hope that our lowly bodies will be made like his in glory, and we say:
Lord, you are our life and resurrection.
Christ, Son of the living God, who raised up Lazarus, your friend, from the dead,

—raise up to life and glory the dead whom you have redeemed by your precious blood.

Christ, consoler of those who mourn, you dried the tears of the family of Lazarus, of the widow's son, and the daughter of Jairus,

—comfort those who mourn for the dead.

Christ, Savior, destroy the reign of sin in our earthly bodies, so that just as through sin we deserved punishment,

—so through you we may gain eternal life.

Christ, Redeemer, look on those who have no hope because they do not know you,

—may they receive faith in the resurrection and in the life of the world to come.

You revealed yourself to the blind man who begged for the light of his eyes,

—show your face to the dead who are still deprived of your light.

When at last our earthly home is dissolved,

—give us a home, not of earthly making, but built of eternity in heaven.

Our Father . . .

PRAYER

Lord God,
you are the glory of believers
and the life of the just.

Your Son redeemed us
by dying and rising to life again.
Our brother (sister) N. was faithful
and believed in our own resurrection.
Give to him (her) the joy and blessings
of the life to come.

We ask this through our Lord Jesus Christ,
   your Son,
who lives and reigns with you and the Holy
   Spirit,
one God, for ever and ever.

May the Lord bless us,
protect us from all evil
and bring us to everlasting life.
—Amen.

Appendix—Hymns

ADVENT

On Jordan's Bank

MELODY: Winchester New L. M. MUSIC: *Musikalisches Handbuch*, Hamburg, 1690. TEXT: *Iordanis ora praevia*, Charles Coffin, 1736. TRANSLATOR: John Chandler, 1837, alt.

1 On Jordan's bank the Baptist's cry
Announces that the Lord is nigh;
Awake and hearken, for he brings
Glad tidings of the King of kings.

2 Then cleansed be ev'ry heart from sin,
Make straight the way of God within;
O let us all our hearts prepare
For Christ to come and enter there.

3 For you are man's salvation, Lord,
Our refuge and our great reward;
Once more upon your people shine,
And fill the world with love divine.

4 To God the Son all glory be,
Whose advent set all nations free,
Whom with the Father we adore,
And Holy Spirit ever more.

O Come, O Come, Emmanuel

MELODY: Veni, Veni Emmanuel L. M. with Refrain. MUSIC: Thomas Helmore, 1811–1890, adapted from a first Mode Responsory in a 15th century French *Processional*. TEXT: *Veni, Veni Emmanuel*, a paraphrase of the Latin 12th-13th century "Great O Antiphons" in *Psalteriolum Cantionum Catholicarum*, 1770. TRANSLATOR: John Mason Neale, 1818–1886, et al.

1 O come, O come, Emmanuel,
And ransom captive Israel,
That mourns in lonely exile here
Until the Son of God appear.

Refrain:

Rejoice! Rejoice! O Israel
To thee shall come Emmanuel!

2 O come, thou wisdom, from on high,
And order all things far and nigh;
To us the path of knowledge show,
And teach us in her ways to go.

Refrain

3 O come, O come, thou Lord of might,
Who to thy tribes on Sinai's height
In ancient times did give the law,
In cloud, and majesty, and awe.

Refrain

4 O come, thou rod of Jesse's stem,
From ev'ry foe deliver them
That trust thy mighty power to save,
And give them vict'ry o'er the grave.

Refrain

5 O come, thou key of David, come,
   And open wide our heav'nly home,
   Make safe the way that leads on high,
   That we no more have cause to sigh.
                    Refrain

6 O come, thou Dayspring from on high,
   And cheer us by thy drawing nigh;
   Disperse the gloomy clouds of night
   And death's dark shadow put to flight.
                    Refrain

7 O come, Desire of nations, bind
   In one the hearts of all mankind;
   Bid every strife and quarrel cease
   And fill the world with heaven's peace.
                    Refrain

CHRISTMAS

O Come, All Ye Faithful

MELODY: Adeste Fideles Irregular with Refrain. MUSIC: J. F. Wade, 1711–1786.
TEXT: J. F. Wade, *Adeste Fideles*, Latin, 18th century. TRANSLATOR: Frederick
Oakeley, 1841, et al.

1 O come, all ye faithful, joyful and triumphant,
   O come ye, O come ye to Bethlehem;
   Come and behold him, born the King of angels;

Refrain:

   O come, let us adore him,
   O come, let us adore him,
   O come, let us adore him,
   Christ the Lord.

2 Sing, choirs of angels, sing in exultation,
   Sing, all ye citizens of heaven above;
   Glory to God, in the highest glory:

Refrain

3 Savior, we greet thee, born this happy morning,
   Jesus, to thee be all glory giv'n;
   Word of the Father, now in flesh appearing:

Refrain

Sion, Sing

MELODY: Sion, Sing Irregular with Antiphon. MUSIC: Lucien Deiss, C. S. Sp., 1965. TEXT: Lucien Deiss, C. S. Sp., 1969.

1   Rise and shine forth, for your light has come,
 And upon you breaks the glory of the Lord:
 For the darkness covers the earth,
 And the thick clouds, the people.

Antiphon:

Sion, sing, break into song!
For within you is the Lord
With his saving power.

2   But upon you the Lord shall dawn,
 And in you his splendor shall be revealed;
 Your light shall guide the Gentiles on their path,
 And kings shall walk in your brightness.

Antiphon

3   Wonder and thanksgiving shall fill your heart,
 As the wealth of nations enriches you;
 You shall be called the City of the Lord,
 Dear to the Holy One of Israel.

Antiphon

4   You who were desolate and alone,
 A place unvisited by men,
 Shall be the pride of ages untold,
 And everlasting joy to the nations.

Antiphon

5 No more shall the sun be your light by day,
Nor the moon's beam enlighten you by night;
The Lord shall be your everlasting light,
And your God shall be your glory.

Antiphon

6 No more for you the setting of suns,
No more the waning of moons;
The Lord shall be your everlasting light,
And the days of your mourning shall come to an
end.

Antiphon

LENT

Lord Who Throughout These Forty Days

MELODY: Saint Flavian, C. M. MUSIC: Adapted from *Psalm 132*, John Day's *Psalter*, 1562. TEXT: Claudia Hernaman, 1838–1898, alt.

1 Lord, who throughout these forty days
   For us did fast and pray,
   Teach us with you to mourn our sins,
   And close by you to stay.

2 As you with Satan did contend
   And did the vict'ry win,
   O give us strength in you to fight,
   In you to conquer sin.

3 As you did hunger and did thirst,
   So teach us, gracious Lord,
   To die to self and so to live
   By your most holy word.

4 Abide with us, that through this life
   Of suff'ring and of pain
   An Easter of unending joy
   We may at last attain.

Draw Near, O Lord

MELODY: Attende Domine 11.11.11 with Refrain. MUSIC: *Paris Processional*, 1824. TEXT: *Attende Domine*. Translator: Melvin Farrell, S. S.

1 O King exalted, Savior of all nations,
See how our grieving lifts our eyes to heaven;
Hear us, Redeemer, as we beg forgiveness.

Refrain:

Draw near, O Lord, our God, graciously hear us,
guilty of sinning before you.

2 Might of the Father, Keystone of God's temple,
Way of salvation, Gate to heaven's glory;
Sin has enslaved us; free your sons from bondage.

Refrain

3 We pray you, O God, throned in strength and splendor,
Hear from your kingdom this, our song of sorrow:
Show us your mercy, pardon our offenses.

Refrain

4 Humbly confessing countless sins committed,
Our hearts are broken, laying bare their secrets;
Cleanse us, Redeemer, boundless in compassion.

Refrain

5 Innocent captive, unresisting victim,
Liars denounced you, sentenced for the guilty;
Once you redeemed us: now renew us, Jesus.

Refrain

EASTER

Alleluia! The Strife Is O'er

MELODY: Vistory 8.8.8 with Alleluias. MUSIC: G. P. da Palestrina, 1588, ad. with alleluias by W. H. Monk, 1861. TEXT: *Symphonia Sirenum Selectarum*, Cologne, 1695. TRANSLATOR: Francis Pott, 1861, alt.

1 Alleluia! Alleluia! Alleluia!
  The strife is o'er, the battle done;
  Now is the Victor's triumph won:
  O let the song of praise be sung.
  Alleluia!

2 Alleluia! Alleluia! Alleluia!
  On the third morn he rose again,
  Glorious in majesty to reign:
  O let us swell the joyful strain:
  Alleluia!

3 Alleluia! Alleluia! Alleluia!
  O risen Lord, all praise to thee,
  Who from our sin has set us free,
  That we may live eternally:
  Alleluia!

Ye Sons and Daughters

MELODY: O Filii Et Filiae, 8.8.8 with Alleluias. MUSIC: 17th century French Proper Melody. TEXT: *O filii et filiae,* Jean Tisserand, d. 1474. Translator: John Mason Neale, 1818–1866, alt.

1 Alleluia, alleluia, alleluia.
Ye sons and daughters, let us sing!
The King of heav'n, the glorious King,
O'er death today rose triumphing.
Alleluia!

2 Alleluia, alleluia, alleluia.
That Easter morn, at break of day,
The faithful women went their way
To seek the tomb where Jesus lay.
Alleluia!

3 Alleluia, alleluia, alleluia.
An angel clad in white they see,
Who sat, and spoke unto the three,
"Your Lord doth go to Galilee."
Alleluia!

4 Alleluia, alleluia, alleluia.
On this most holy day of days,
To God your hearts and voices raise,
In laud and jubilee and praise.
Alleluia!

5 Alleluia, alleluia, alleluia.
And we with Holy Church unite,
As evermore is just and right,
In glory to the King of light.
Alleluia!

PENTECOST

Come, Holy Ghost

MELODY: Tallis Ordinal, CM. TEXT ATTRIBUTED to Rabanus Maurus, 766–856.
TRANSLATOR: Anonymous.

1   Come, Holy Ghost, Creator blest,
And in our hearts take up thy rest;
Come with thy grace and heavenly aid,
To fill the hearts which thou hast made,
To fill the hearts which thou hast made.

2   O Comforter, to thee we cry,
Thou gift of God sent from on high,
Thou font of life and fire of love,
The soul's anointing from above,
The soul's anointing from above.

3   Praise be to thee, Father and Son,
And Holy Spirit, with them One;
And may the Son on us bestow
All gifts that from the Spirit flow,
All gifts that from the Spirit flow.

ORDINARY TIME

Morning Has Broken

MELODY: Bunessan 55.54.D. MUSIC: Old Gaelic Melody. TEXT: Eleanor Farjeon, 1881–1965.

1 Morning has broken
   Like the first morning,
   Blackbird has spoken
   Like the first bird.
   Praise for the singing!
   Praise for the morning!
   Praise for them, springing
   Fresh from the Word!

2 Sweet the rains new fall
   Sunlit from heaven,
   Like the first dew fall
   On the first grass.
   Praise for the sweetness
   Of the wet garden,
   Sprung in completeness
   Where his feet pass.

3 Mine is the sunlight!
   Mine is the morning,
   Born of the one light
   Eden saw play!
   Praise with elation,

Praise every morning,
God's re-creation
Of the new day!

God Father, Praise and Glory

MELODY: Gott Vater! Sei Gepriesen 76.76 with Refrain. MUSIC: *Mainz Gesangbuch*, 1833. TEXT: Anon. TRANSLATOR: John Rothensteiner, 1936, alt.

1 God Father, praise and glory
Your children come to sing.
Good will and peace to mankind,
The gifts your kingdom brings.

Refrain:

O most Holy Trinity,
Undivided Unity;
Holy God, Mighty God,
God Immortal, be adored.

2 And you, Lord Coeternal,
God's sole begotten Son,
O Jesus, King anointed,
You have redemption won.

Refrain

3 O Holy Ghost, Creator,
The Gift of God most high,
Life, love and holy wisdom,
Our weakness now supply.

Refrain

Holy, Holy, Holy

Melody: Nicaea 11. 12. 12. 10. Music: John B. Dykes, 1823–1876. Text: Reginald
Heber, 1783–1826, alt.

1 Holy, holy, holy! Lord God Almighty!
   Early in the morning our song shall rise to thee:
   Holy, holy, holy! Merciful and mighty,
   God in three persons, blessed Trinity.

2 Holy, holy, holy! All the saints adore thee,
   Though the eye of sinful man thy glory may not see;
   Only thou art holy; there is none beside thee,
   Which were, and are, and ever more shall be.

3 Holy, holy, holy! Lord God Almighty!
   All thy works shall praise thy name, in earth, and
       sky, and sea;
   Holy, holy, holy! Merciful and mighty,
   God in three persons, blessed Trinity.

All Hail, Adored Trinity

MELODY: Old 100th L.M. MUSIC: Attributed to Louis Bourgeois, 1516–1561. Melody of *Psalm 134* in the *Genevan Psalter,* 1551, with English (1583) form of rhythm in last line. TEXTS: Sts. 1, 2, 3, *Ave, colenda Trinitas,* anon. before 11th century; st. 4, *Praise God,* Thomas Ken, 1709. TRANSLATOR: J. D. Chambers, 1805–1893, cento, alt.

1 All hail, adored Trinity:
All praise, eternal Unity:
O God the Father, God the Son,
And God the Spirit, ever One.

2 Three Persons praise we evermore,
And thee the Eternal One adore:
In thy sure mercy, ever kind,
May we our true protection find.

3 O Trinity, O Unity,
Be present as we worship thee;
And to the angels' songs in light
Our prayers and praises now unite.

4 Praise God, from whom all blessings flow;
Praise him, all creatures here below;
Praise him above, ye heav'nly host:
Praise Father, Son, and Holy Ghost.

From All That Dwell Below the Skies

MELODY: Erschienen Ist Der Herrliche Tag L.M. with Hallelujah. MUSIC: Nikolaus Hermann, 1560. TEXT: Isaac Watts, 1719.

MELODY: Eisenach L.M. MUSIC: Johann H. Schein, 1583–1630. TEXT: Isaac Watts, 1719.

1 From all that dwell below the skies
Let the Creator's praise arise:
Let the Redeemer's name be sung
Through every land, by every tongue,
Hallelujah!

2 Eternal are thy mercies, Lord;
Eternal truth attends thy word:
Thy praise shall sound from shore to shore,
Till suns shall rise and set no more:
Hallelujah!

ORDINARY TIME

Now Thank We All Our God

MELODY: Nun Danket 67.67.66.66. MUSIC: Johann Crüger, 1598–1662. TEXT: Based on *Ecclesiasticus 50:22–24*, Martin Rinkart, 1586–1649. TRANSLATOR: Catherine Winkworth, 1829–1878.

1   Now thank we all our God
    With heart and hands and voices,
    Who wondrous things has done,
    In whom his world rejoices;
    Who from our mothers' arms
    Has blessed us on our way
    With countless gifts of love,
    And still is ours today.

2   O may this gracious God
    Through all our life be near us,
    With ever joyful hearts,
    And blessed peace to cheer us;
    Preserve us in his grace,
    And guide us in distress,
    And free us from all sin,
    Till heaven we possess.

3   All praise and thanks to God
    The Father now be given,
    The Son and Spirit blest,
    Who reigns in highest heaven;
    Eternal, Triune God,
    Whom earth and heaven adore;
    For thus it was, is now,
    And shall be ever more.

Let All Things Now Living

MELODY: The Ash Grove 6.6.11.6.6.11D. MUSIC: Traditional Welsh Melody. TEXT: Anon.

1 Let all things now living a song of thanksgiving
To God our Creator triumphantly raise;
Who fashioned and made us, protected and stayed
  us,
Who guideth us on to the end of our days.
His banners are o'er us, his light goes before us,
A pillar of fire shining forth in the night:
Till shadows have vanished and darkness is ban-
  ished,
As forward we travel from light into Light.

2 His law he enforces, the stars in their courses,
The sun in his orbit obediently shine,
The hills and the mountains, the rivers and foun-
  tains,
The depths of the ocean proclaim him divine.
We, too, should be voicing our love and rejoicing
With glad adoration, a song let us raise:
Till all things now living unite in thanksgiving,
To God in the highest, hosanna and praise.

Father We Thank Thee

MELODY: Rendez à Dieu 98.98.D. MUSIC: Louis Bourgeois, 1543. TEXT: Didache,
c. 110. TRANSLATOR: F. Bland Tucker.

1 Father, we thank thee who hast planted
   Thy holy Name within our hearts.
   Knowledge and faith and life immortal
   Jesus, thy Son, to us imparts.
   Thou, Lord, didst make all for thy pleasure,
   Didst give man food for all his days,
   Giving in Christ the Bread eternal;
   Thine is the power, be thine the praise.

2 Watch o'er thy Church, O Lord, in mercy,
   Save it from evil, guard it still;
   Perfect it in thy love, unite it,
   Cleansed and conformed unto thy will.
   As grain, once scattered on the hillsides,
   Was in this broken bread made one,
   So from all lands thy Church be gathered
   Into thy kingdom by thy Son.

Day Is Done

MELODY: Ar Hyd Y Nos 84.84.88.84. MUSIC: Traditional Welsh Melody. TEXT:
James Quinn, S. J.

1   Day is done, but Love unfailing
    Dwells ever here;
    Shadows fall, but hope, prevailing,
    Calms every fear.
    Loving Father, none forsaking,
    Take our hearts, of Love's own making,
    Watch our sleeping, guard our waking,
    Be always near.

2   Dark descends, but Light unending
    Shines through our night;
    You are with us, ever lending
    New strength to sight;
    One in love, your truth confessing,
    One in hope of heaven's blessing,
    May we see, in love's possessing,
    Love's endless light!

3   Eyes will close, but you, unsleeping,
    Watch by our side;
    Death may come: in Love's safe keeping
    Still we abide
    God of love, all evil quelling,
    Sin forgiving, fear dispelling,
    Stay with us, our hearts indwelling;
    This eventide.

O God, Our Help in Ages Past

MELODY: Saint Anne C. M. MUSIC: William Croft, 1708. TEXT: Isaac Watts, 1674–1748, alt.

1 O God, our help in ages past,
Our hope for years to come,
Our shelter from the stormy blast
And our eternal home;

2 Beneath the shadow of your throne
Your saints have dwelt secure;
Sufficient is your arm alone,
And our defense is sure.

3 Before the hills in order stood,
Or earth received her frame,
From everlasting you are God,
To endless years the same.

4 A thousand ages in your sight
Are like an evening gone,
Short as the watch that ends the night
Before the rising sun.

5 Time, like an ever-rolling stream,
Bears all its sons away;
They fly forgotten, as a dream
Dies at the opening day.

6 O God, our help in ages past,
Our hope for years to come,
Be now our guide while life shall last,
And our eternal home.

O Radiant Light, O Sun Divine

MELODY: Jesu, Dulcis Memoria (plainchant) L. M. MUSIC: Gregorian. TEXT: *Phos Hilaron*, Greek 3rd century. TRANSLATOR: William G. Storey.

1 O radiant Light, O sun divine
   Of God the Father's deathless face,
   O image of the light sublime
   That fills the heav'nly dwelling place.

2 Lord Jesus Christ, as daylight fades,
   As shine the lights of eventide,
   We praise the Father with the Son,
   The Spirit blest and with them one.

3 O Son of God, the source of life,
   Praise is your due by night and day;
   Unsullied lips must raise the strain
   Of your proclaimed and splendid name.

IN HONOR OF THE BLESSED VIRGIN MARY

Sing of Mary

TEXT: Roland F. Palmer.

1 Sing of Mary, pure and lowly,
Virgin mother undefiled,
Sing of God's own son most holy,
Who became her little child.
Fairest child of fairest mother,
God the Lord who came to earth,
Word made flesh, our very brother,
Takes our nature by his birth.

2 Sing of Jesus, son of Mary,
In the home at Nazareth.
Toil and labor cannot weary
Love enduring unto death.
Constant was the love he gave her,
Though he went forth from her side,
Forth to preach, and heal, and suffer,
Till on Calvary he died.

3 Joyful Mother, full of gladness,
In your arms, your Lord was borne.
Mournful Mother, full of sadness,
All your heart with pain was torn.
Glorious Mother, now rewarded,
With a crown at Jesus' hand,
Age to age your name recorded
Shall be blest in every land.

4 Glory be to God the Father;
  Glory be to God the Son;
  Glory be to God the Spirit;
  Glory to the Three in One.
  From the heart of blessed Mary,
  From all saints the song ascends;
  And the Church the strain re-echoes
  Unto earth's remotest ends.

FOR THE DEAD.

For All the Saints

MELODY: Sine Nomine 10.10.10 with Alleluias. MUSIC: Ralph Vaughan Williams, 1872–1958. TEXT: William W. How, 1823–1897.

1 For all the saints who from their labors rest,
Who thee by faith before the world confessed,
Thy name, O Jesus, be for ever blest: Alleluia, alleluia!

2 Thou wast their rock, their fortress and their might;
Thou, Lord, their captain in the well-fought fight;
Thou in the darkness drear their one true light:
Alleluia, alleluia!

3 O blest communion, fellowship divine!
We feebly struggle, they in glory shine,
Yet all are one in thee, for all are thine:
Alleluia, alleluia!

4 But, lo, there breaks a yet more glorious day;
The saints triumphant rise in bright array:
The King of glory passes on his way:
Alleluia, alleluia!

Music from *The English Hymnal* by permission of Oxford University Press.

The Morning and Evening Prayers offered in this volume are excerpts from the complete Liturgy of the Hours.

ADVENT:
—Morning Prayer: Advent, 2nd Week, Thursday
 Evening Prayer: Advent, 3rd Week, Dec. 18, Thursday
—Morning Prayer: Advent, 3rd Week, Dec. 18, Tuesday
 Evening Prayer: Advent, 3rd Week, Dec. 22, Wednesday

CHRISTMAS:
—Morning Prayer: Christmas
 Evening Prayer: Christmas

LENT:
—Morning Prayer: Lent, 4th Sunday
 Evening Prayer: Lent, 4th Sunday
—Morning Prayer: Lent, 2nd Week, Monday
 Evening Prayer: Lent, 2nd Week, Monday
—Morning Prayer: Lent, 2nd Week, Friday
 Evening Prayer: Lent, 2nd Week, Friday

EASTER:
—Morning Prayer: Easter
 Evening Prayer: Easter
—Morning Prayer: Easter Season, 2nd Week, Saturday
 Evening Prayer: Third Sunday of Easter

PENTECOST:
—Morning Prayer: Pentecost
 Evening Prayer: Pentecost

ORDINARY TIME:
 Week I, (Sunday Morning Prayer: Canticle of Zechariah and prayers from Eighth Sunday in Ordinary Time; Saturday Evening Prayer: Canticle of Mary and prayers from Eleventh Sunday in Ordinary Time).

In Honor of the Blessed Virgin:
 Common of the Blessed Virgin

For the Dead:
 —Morning Prayer: Office for the Dead
 Evening Prayer: Office for the Dead